Totally WASHi!

MORE THAN 45 Super Cute WASHI TAPE CRAFTS * FOR KIDS *

Ashley Ann Laz

Adamsmedia
Avon, Massachusetts

Published by
Adams Media, a division of F+W Media, Inc.
57 Littlefield Street, Avon, MA 02322. U.S.A.
www.adamsmedia.com

ISBN 10: 1-4405-7941-5
ISBN 13: 978-1-4405-7941-7
eISBN 10: 1-4405-7942-3
eISBN 13: 978-1-4405-7942-4

Printed by RR Donnelley, Salem, VA, U.S.A.

10   9   8   7   6   5   4   3   2

August 2014

Library of Congress Cataloging-in-Publication Data

Laz, Ashley Ann.
  Totally washi! / Ashley Ann Laz.
     pages cm
  Includes bibliographical references and index.
  ISBN-13: 978-1-4405-7941-7 (pb)
  ISBN-10: 1-4405-7941-5 (pb)
  ISBN-13: 978-1-4405-7942-4 (ebook)
  ISBN-10: 1-4405-7942-3 (ebook)
1. Tape craft. 2. Gummed paper tape. 3. Japanese paper. I. Title.
  TT869.7.L39 2014
  745.5--dc23
              2014008243

Readers are urged to take all appropriate precautions before undertaking any how-to task. Always read and follow instructions and safety warnings for all tools and materials, and call in a professional if the task stretches your abilities too far. Although every effort has been made to provide the best possible information in this book, neither the publisher nor the author is responsible for accidents, injuries, or damage incurred as a result of tasks undertaken by readers. This book is not a substitute for professional services.

Many of the designations used by manufacturers and sellers to distinguish their product are claimed as trademarks. Where those designations appear in this book and F+W Media, Inc. was aware of a trademark claim, the designations have been printed with initial capital letters.

Photos by Ashley Ann Laz and Adams Media.
Cover design by Erin Alexander.
Cover images © Ashley Ann Laz, Adams Media, 123RF © afe207.

This book is available at quantity discounts for bulk purchases.
For information, please call 1-800-289-0963.

Acknowledgments

I would like to thank my mother, Dianna, for her unending support and for being a constant source of inspiration. A special thanks to Zoe, Tatiana, and Nicole for their enthusiasm and all the help they offered throughout this process. I'd also like to give a big thanks to Henry Soto, Cristopher Laz, and of course, you, the reader!

Contents

Introduction

WELCOME TO THE AWESOME WORLD OF WASHI TAPE! What is washi tape, you ask? It's a specialty tape that's made from washi paper, a handmade all-natural Japanese paper. It feels almost like masking tape—but a very pretty, colorful masking tape. It comes in so many beautiful prints, unique colors, and cool patterns. All these options make it perfect for whipping up some amazing DIY projects for you and your friends!

Here are some of the best things about washi tape:

* You can decorate almost any surface with it, since it's removable and doesn't leave that gross sticky stuff behind.
* If you change your mind after you decorate something, you can change it, remove it, or start all over again.
* It doesn't cost too much, so you can afford to buy lots of patterns, create multiple versions of your favorite projects, and make cool gifts without spending a ton of cash!
* You can find washi tape practically anywhere—in most craft stores, online, and in small stationery boutiques. There are even websites starting to appear that will allow you to design your own washi tapes.

Time for a quick history lesson! *Washi* is the Japanese word for paper, *wa* meaning "Japanese" and *shi* meaning "paper." Paper began to be made in Japan in the year A.D. 610.

Washi paper is usually made from all-natural fibers, such as from the bark of the gampi tree, the mitsumata shrub, or the paper mulberry (kozo), but can also be made using materials you've probably heard of, like bamboo, hemp, rice, and wheat. The paper has been used throughout history for all kinds of things, including art, clothing, food (but duh—don't eat the paper you buy at the store, though!), furniture, weaponry, toys, and even umbrellas. Traditional washi paper is made by hand, but as papermaking technology became more advanced, other methods have been used. In 2006 a low-tack acrylic glue was added to the back of the paper, and there you have it—washi tape was born!

In this book, you and your friends will find so many super cute ways to use washi tape . . .

* Love personalized jewelry? The Initial Necklace is a must-have.
* Tired of your boring plastic phone cover? Make yourself a washi tape version! Better yet, make a few different ones and switch them out to match your outfits.
* Is your mom's desk a mess? Make her some drawer organizers for her birthday.
* You know you can nail that biology exam. Bring some washi tape–covered pens and pencils you've decorated for you and your lab partner for extra luck on test day.

See? The possibilities are endless. Plus washi tape is so easy to use, you can't mess up these projects! You can follow my directions exactly, or use them as a guideline and customize however you want. Grab some friends, some cool rolls of washi tape, and let's get going!

CHAPTER 1

For You and Your Friends

WHAT IS MORE FUN than getting together with friends and working on crafts together? Whether you're having a sleepover, facing a boring Saturday afternoon, or celebrating a birthday, these projects are perfect for doing with your BFFs.

Let's face it, those storebought jewelry-making kits are so expensive—plus, you're limited to the design options they give you. With washi tape, you don't need to spend tons of money to make your own cute accessories, and you can choose your own colors and patterns!

In this chapter, you will find tons of great ideas for decorating your electronics, as well as instructions for how to create your own unique jewelry and accessories. You can quickly customize all of these ideas to create something that matches your personal style. Retro? Sporty? Sophisticated? Bold? You name it, you can make it! So, what are you waiting for? Let's get started!

Laptop Sleeve

If you are the kind of person who likes to change things up all the time, then this project is perfect for you! You can use this same technique to cover practically any electronic device, like a tablet or iPad. With only a few materials, you can create an awesome cover that shows off your favorite colors and patterns.

MATERIALS:

Posterboard

Pencil

Ruler

Scissors

Washi tape

Magnetic dots (optional)

1. Wrap the posterboard over your electronic device to get a measurement for the cover. The posterboard should fit around your electronic device twice. It should wrap around the device like a book cover with a few inches of extra space on the ends.

2. Using your pencil and ruler, create an outline of where you should cut the posterboard to fit your device. Leave about one inch on each side just in case you make any mistakes!

3. Once you have measured the posterboard, cut out the part you are going to use.

4. Cover the posterboard with washi tape. Make sure you wrap around the front and back of the posterboard you just cut. You can alternate between different colors and patterns of washi tape for a unique design.

5. Add some self-adhesive magnetic dots on the inside of the cover to create a closure for your cover (optional). The magnetic dots will keep the device from sliding out.

6. All done! Now you have a totally unique design for your electronic device.

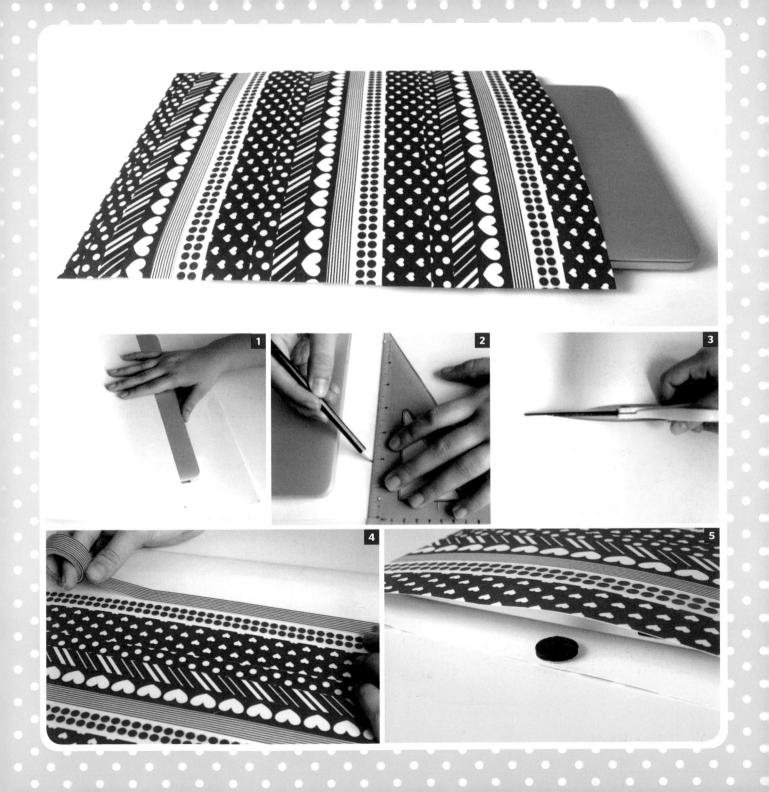

Phone Case Cover

Turn your phone case from drab to fab in just a few easy steps! It is so easy and fun to make your own custom case using just a few pieces of washi tape and a blank case. The possibilities are endless! You can make a bunch of different ones to match your outfit, or even the season.

MATERIALS:

Blank phone case

Damp cloth

Washi tape

Scissors

Glitter or stickers

Superglue (optional)

Rubber gloves (optional)

Mod Podge

Brush

TRY THIS!

There are many ways to spice up this basic design, so don't feel limited to using only washi tape. Try adding studs, rhinestones, glitter, feathers, or stickers to make the case your own.

Continued ➡

1. Completely wipe the surface of your phone case with a damp cloth and let dry.

2. In my example, I used three different tape designs. To follow my pattern, grab your first tape design and start laying strips of tape in whatever direction you'd like. Then add the other types of tape—mix it up by using different colors and patterns.

3. Fold the tape over the edges of the case, and trim the excess washi tape using a pair of scissors.

4. Now you can add any extra embellishments like glitter or stickers. Use a superglue to add any extra design elements to the case. Superglue can get messy; make sure to wear rubber gloves if you use it, protect your workspace with newspaper, and be careful not to spill or drip the glue.

5. To seal and protect the design, brush Mod Podge over your case and embellishments. Allow the case to dry for a few hours between coats. The number of coats may vary between cases. Normally, 2 or 3 coats are perfect for a shiny and smooth surface.

6. Once the final coat of Mod Podge is dry, your case is ready to use!

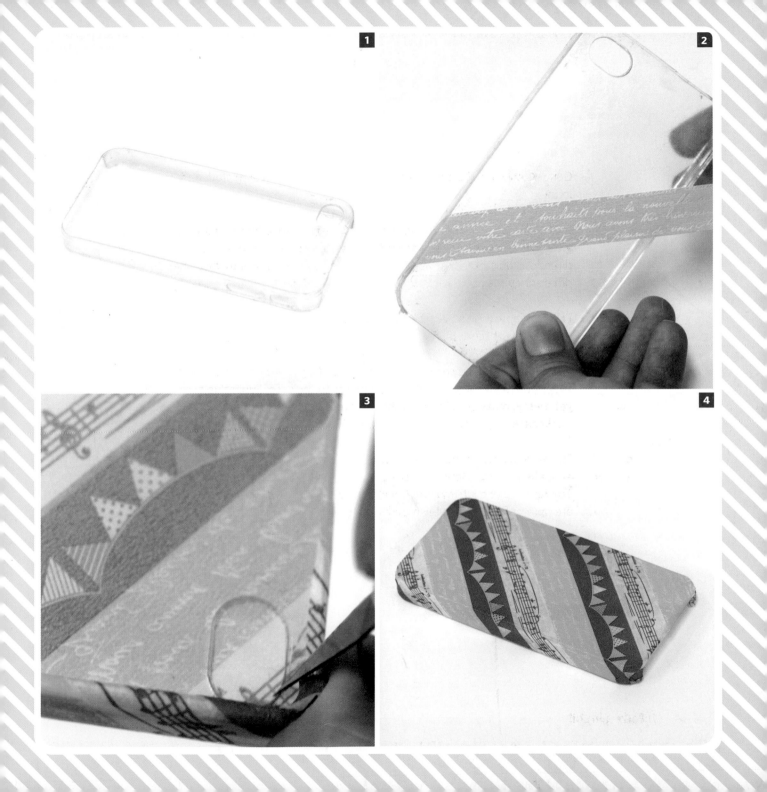

Bookmark

Love reading? Whether it's a book for English class or just for fun, you need to know where you left off. Try creating bookmarks for all of the books you are currently reading, and it will definitely make reading and studying more fun. You can even customize them with quotes from your favorite books for an extra personal touch. This project is so easy that you can whip up a whole bunch of them in no time!

MATERIALS:

Scissors
Ruler
Posterboard
Washi tape
Hole punch (optional)
Ribbon (optional)

1. Measure and cut out a 6" × 2" piece of posterboard. This is the base of your bookmark.

2. Start layering pieces of washi tape on the bookmark. Try creating different effects by layering the pieces diagonally, vertically, or horizontally.

3. This step is optional. If you'd like a little extra customization, you can punch a hole at the top of the bookmark, and loop a ribbon through the hole.

4. Your bookmark is now ready to use!

Washi Bead Necklace

Jewelry can add style to any outfit. But buying tons of necklaces can cost a lot of money, and sometimes it's hard to find the exact color you're looking for. Luckily, creating a stylish necklace is easy with washi tape. You can make your own beads, and try out tons of cool color combinations. Wear a different one with each of your outfits, or wear your favorite one every day. You can also try experimenting with different paper shapes to create different patterns and styles.

MATERIALS:

Ruler
Card stock
Scissors
Washi tape
Necklace chain
Pencil

1. Cut a small strip of card stock. It should measure roughly ½" × 2". Most washi tapes are ½" wide, but you can adjust the size of the paper to fit the width of your washi tape if you need to.

2. Wrap the narrow edge of the strip of paper around a pencil. This step makes it easier to place the washi tape, and gives the paper its "bead" shape.

3. Once you have wrapped the card stock around the pencil, you can wrap your washi tape around it to create the bead. You only need to wrap it around once, but if you don't want to be able to see through the tape, wrap it around a few more times.

4. Cut the excess tape and remove your bead from the pencil. Repeat steps 1 through 4 to create plenty of beads to fill your necklace. Use any combination of tape you choose.

5. String the beads you created onto your necklace in a pattern you like.

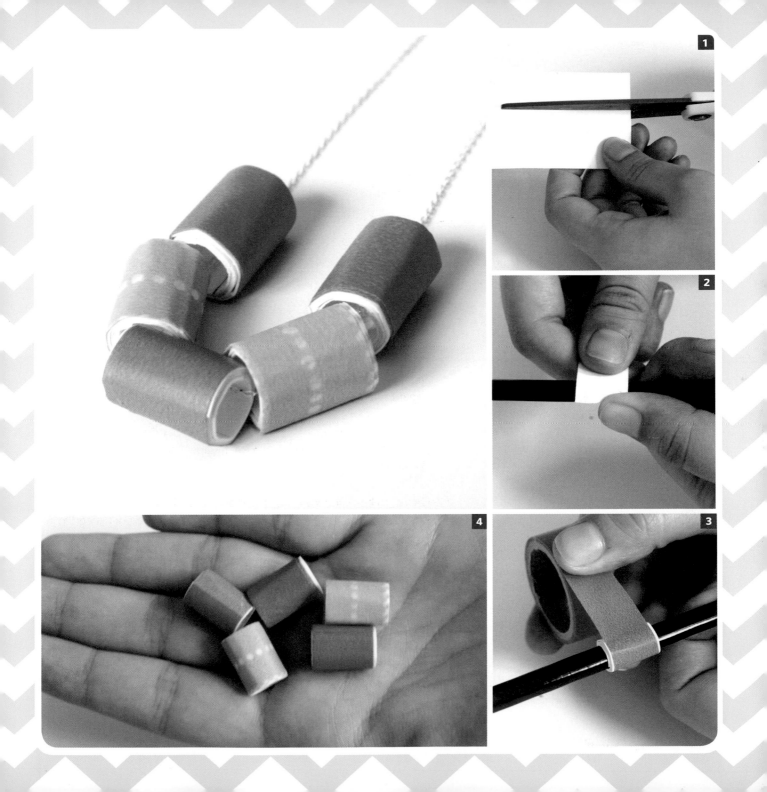

Initial Necklace

Personalized accessories are always in style. But skip the overpriced mall versions and make this monogrammed pendant necklace at home. Actually, create a bunch and give them to your friends and family. You can change the font of the letter using different stickers, and experiment with cool backgrounds. If necklaces aren't your style, try adding the pendant to a keychain instead!

MATERIALS:

Card stock

Scissors

Washi tape

Large hole punch, with a cool shape (or scissors)

Small regular hole punch (the circle kind)

Alphabet stickers

Mod Podge Dimensional Magic

Paper clip or toothpick

Jump ring

Necklace chain

1. Start by cutting out a piece of card stock big enough to be able to punch out the design with your shape hole punch at least once.

2. Layer some pieces of washi tape on the piece of card stock you just cut. Since the pendant will be relatively small, sticking with only one kind of tape may look the best.

Continued ➡

MOD PODGE?

Mod Podge is a great sealer for all types of arts and crafts projects. You can find it in the craft glue section of most craft stores. Look for Mod Podge Dimensional Magic to add a cool 3D effect to your project!

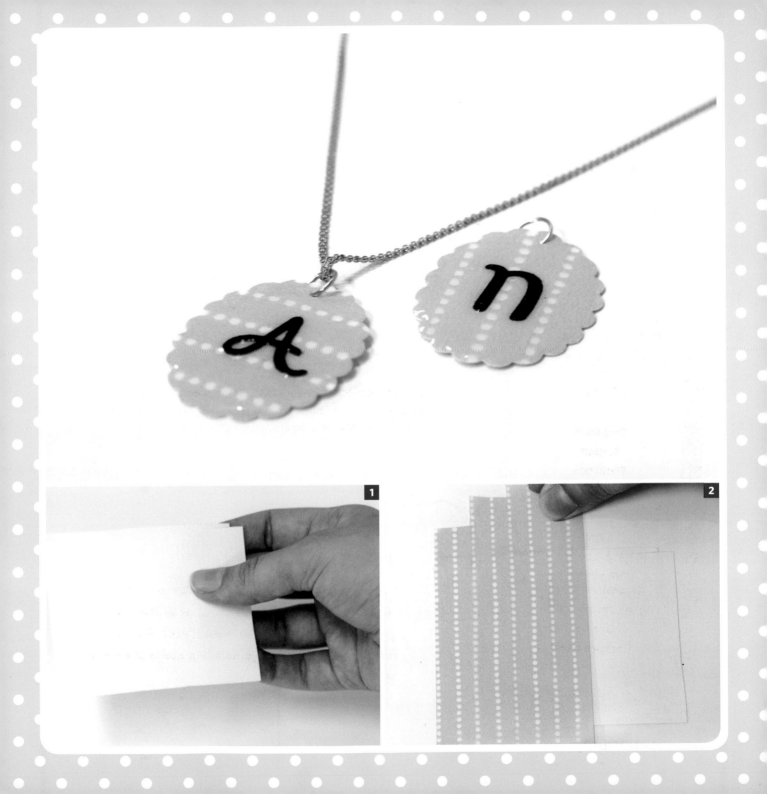

3. Now, punch out one (or more) shapes with the shape hole punch. If you don't have a hole punch that fits the bill, just cut out shapes yourself with a sharp pair of scissors.

4. Add a monogram letter (or any sticker you like!) to the shape for decoration. You can also draw your own letters with 3D paint or markers, if you don't have letter stickers.

5. Cover the pendant with Mod Podge Dimensional Magic. This seals the design so your sticker won't come off, and the shiny finish really makes the pendant pop.

6. Use a paper clip or toothpick to spread the Mod Podge so that it completely covers the sticker, and then allow it to dry for three hours. If you need to add another layer, apply it before moving on to the next step, and allow it to dry.

7. Use the smaller regular hole punch to create a hole at the top of the pendant for the jump ring (that's the metal circle that'll connect the pendant to the necklace chain).

8. Loop your jump ring through the pendant.

9. Finally, thread your newly created pendant on a necklace chain.

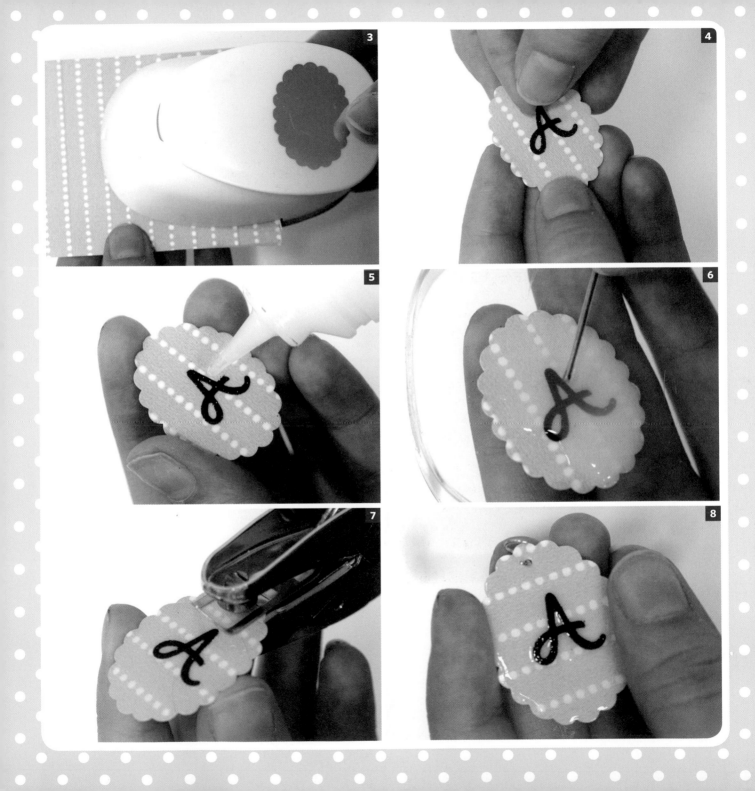

Braided Friendship Bracelet

Most friendship bracelets are made from thread or those little rubber bands. Try a different spin on them using washi tape! These bracelets take less than ten minutes to make. They're a great and simple project to make with your best friends while you're watching a movie. Try making them in your favorite colors, or check the sidebar for some cool color meanings. Just make sure you don't get these bracelets wet!

MATERIALS:

Scissors
Washi tape

Color Meanings!

* Yellow – Happiness
* Blue – Loyalty
* Green – Growth
* Purple – Imagination
* Pink – Love
* Red – Confidence

Continued ➡

1. Pull out a piece of washi tape long enough to wrap around your wrist twice, then fold it onto itself to create a single strand and all of the adhesive is covered.

2. Cut the strand you just folded in half. You should now have two strands of washi tape. Repeat these two steps until you have four strands of washi tape. You'll only need three strands for this project, so put aside the extra strand to use for another bracelet.

3. Line up all three of your strands, and wrap one end with washi tape to keep them all in place while you are braiding. To make it easier, you can tape the end of the strands onto a desk or other surface. Start braiding the strands by looping first the right strand over the center strand, then the left strand over this new center strand. Repeat these two steps, braiding one strand over another in the same pattern.

4. Finish the bracelet by closing the braid with a piece of washi tape. Trim off any extra strands sticking out to make the ends even. Put on your bracelet, and connect the ends together with a piece of washi tape.

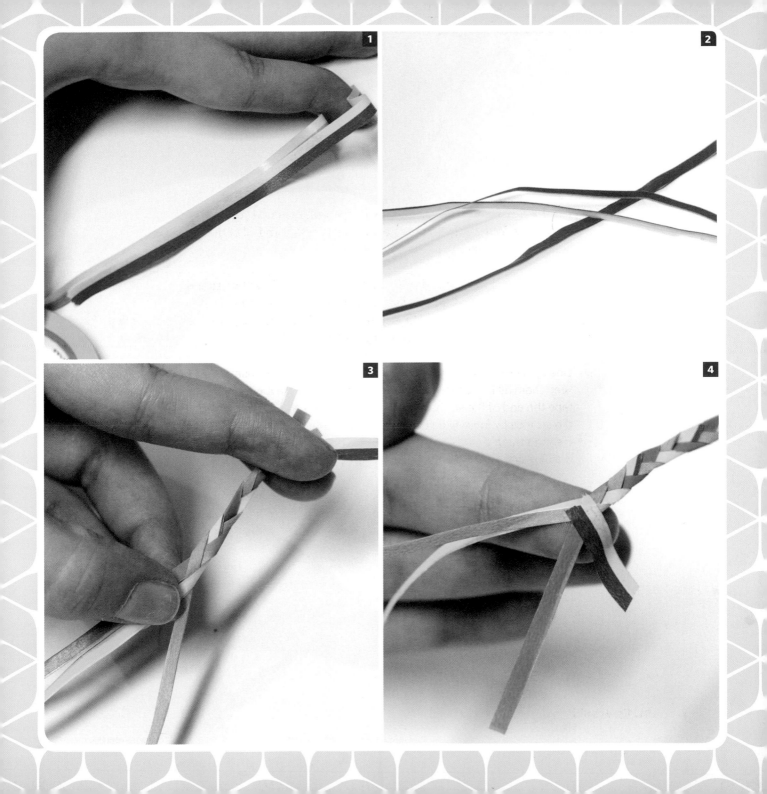

Toilet Paper Roll Bracelet

Who would have thought that a toilet paper roll could actually be fashionable? Since you completely cover the ugly brown roll with washi tape, no one will ever know you used one! Whenever you finish a toilet paper roll, or even a paper towel roll, save it. You can create tons of bangles from only one roll.

MATERIALS:

Toilet paper roll
Scissors
Washi tape
Hole punch
Craft thread

1. Start by making sure your toilet paper roll is clean and free of any toilet paper or adhesive. Don't worry too much about removing every last scrap, as it will all be covered by the tape.

2. Grab your roll, and cut it open from end to end, the long way. Make sure your cut is straight.

3. Once you have cut it vertically, cut a horizontal piece out of the toilet paper roll. This will be the bracelet.

4. Start layering pieces of washi tape over the band you just created. You can layer tape vertically, horizontally, or diagonally—however you like!

5. Using a small hole punch, make a hole at each short end of the band.

6. Loop some craft thread through each hole to close the band, and secure with a loose knot. Make sure the bracelet fits over your hand, adjusting the length of the thread if necessary; tighten the knot, and cut off any extra thread. Now your bracelet is ready to wear.

1

2

3

4

5

6

Popsicle Stick Bracelet

If you're looking for a different kind of bracelet, here's another idea! This type of bracelet is strong enough to hold some extra sparkle—like some rhinestones, glitter, or other embellishments. You can buy craft sticks at a craft supply shop or the dollar store and make them into bracelets in no time.

MATERIALS:

Popsicle or flat craft sticks

Water, pot, tongs

Glasses or mugs

Scissors

Washi tape

Embellishments
(such as markers, glitter, rhinestones, stickers, feathers)

Glue
(if using embellishments)

Mod Podge and brush
(optional)

1. You'll need to soak the wooden Popsicle sticks in water in order for the wood to become pliable enough to bend into a bracelet shape. Put them in a bowl of water and let them soak overnight.

2. The next day, have a parent help you boil water in a pot. Let the sticks soak in the boiling water while the pot is still on the stove for 20–30 minutes to help make them even more pliable.

3. While the sticks are soaking in the boiling water, find a glass or mug that's roughly the same size as your wrist. You're going to use this to form the shape of the bracelet. The wood will stretch a bit to get over your hand, but you don't want to make the bangle too small, as it could crack when you try to slide it on.

4. Have a parent use tongs to remove the Popsicle sticks from the pot one at a time, and place them inside the rim of your chosen glass or cup to be shaped before they cool off. If you wait for the sticks to cool, they will crack when you put them in the cups.

5. Once the Popsicle sticks are completely dry and you do not see any water on them, they should easily slide out of the cups. This can take anywhere from 24–48 hours.

6. Decorate the bent stick bracelets with washi tape by wrapping the tape down the stick. For an extra touch, add your name or a word with markers or pens, or add glitter, rhinestones, or any other decorations. You can seal the design with Mod Podge, if you like.

7. Once it's decorated to your liking, your bracelet is ready to wear!

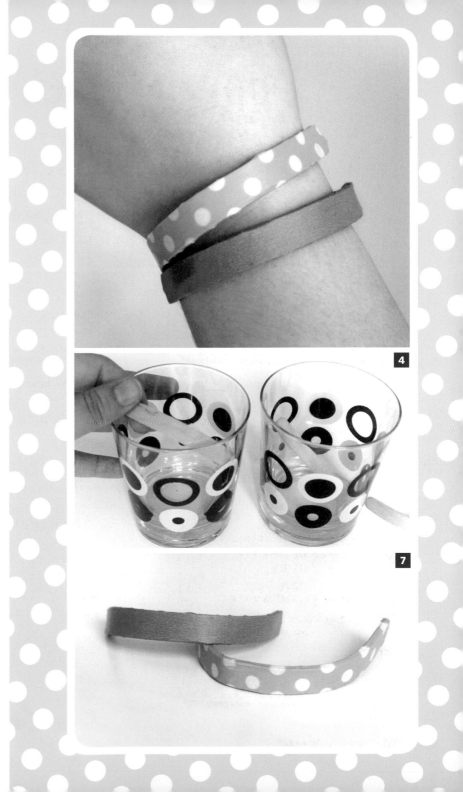

Feather Dangle Earrings

The look of feather earrings is fun and cute, but the retail versions can be really pricey. Making them out of inexpensive, easy-to-find materials can get you the look you need without burning through cash. You can make them to match your school colors, favorite outfit, or make each earring different, for a really quirky look!

MATERIALS:
....

Washi tape

Craft scissors

Hole punch

Earring hooks (2)

Pliers

1. Pull out approximately 2" of washi tape. (The measurement doesn't need to be exact.)

2. Fold the washi tape back onto itself so that all the adhesive is covered, making sure to press out any creases or bubbles. Cut off the folded piece.

3. Repeat these steps with another piece of washi tape. Once you have two folded strips, you can move on.

Continued ➡

TRY THIS!

To up the cool factor of these earrings, try adding beads or using real feathers from a craft store.

4. If you want the feathers to be the same size, stack the two pieces of folded tape on top of each other and fold them lengthwise (the long way).

5. Cut a half-oval shape on the folded washi tape with your scissors, making sure you cut through both pieces.

6. When you unfold the pieces of tape, you should have two oval shapes.

7. Fold the pieces of tape back in and make a bunch of short cuts on the sides. If you don't want the cuts to be even, you can freehand the cuts, or you can use a pencil to mark the areas you would like to cut.

8. Unfold your washi tape, and you should now have two cute little feathers! Separate each cut with your fingers to make the pieces stick out more.

9. Next, grab the small hole punch and make a hole at the top of the "feather." If you don't have a hole punch, you can carefully puncture a small hole with a pen or the tip of your scissors.

10. Finally, loop an earring hook through the hole you just made. The feather should slip onto the earring hook easily, but for extra security you can use pliers to adjust the earring hook open, and then to close it again. Now your earrings are ready to wear!

Stud Earrings

When it comes to accessories, sometimes simplicity is best. Stud earrings are perfect for daily use. Unlike dangle earrings, studs won't get caught in anything, and they aren't too heavy on your ears. A huge plus is that you can make these earrings quickly in a bunch of different colors to match any of your outfits. These studs are also a great handmade gift for you to give friends and family.

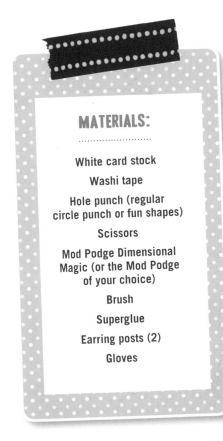

MATERIALS:

White card stock

Washi tape

Hole punch (regular circle punch or fun shapes)

Scissors

Mod Podge Dimensional Magic (or the Mod Podge of your choice)

Brush

Superglue

Earring posts (2)

Gloves

1. First, cut a strip of card stock. Size isn't too important—just make sure you have enough space to punch or cut out your designs.

2. Place strips of washi tape over the card stock. The white card stock makes the washi tape designs brighter and easier to see.

3. Punch holes in the washi tape–covered card stock strip with your hole punch. If you don't have a hole punch, try creating designs freehand with scissors.

4. Since you might be wearing the earrings daily, you want to make sure the washi tape will not rip or get damaged. To protect the pattern, seal the design with Dimensional Magic or any Mod Podge finish you prefer. Allow the designs to dry for a few hours.

5. Once the shapes are dry, grab some superglue and attach them to your earring posts. Superglue can be really messy—and sticky!—so make sure you protect your work area with newspaper, wear gloves, and be careful not to spill any glue.

6. Allow the superglue to dry for at least 30 minutes, and your designs are ready to wear! These stud earrings should be okay for swimming and showers as long as you use a sealer like Modge Podge—but to be extra cautious, remove them before going into the water.

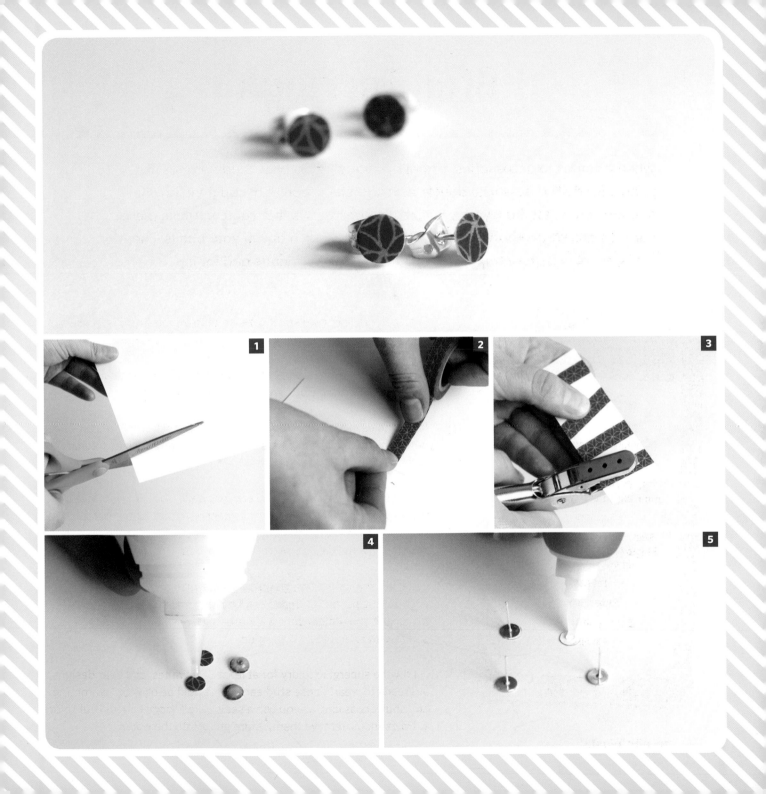

Bobby Pin Flower

Natural flowers are beautiful to wear in your hair, but they can be hard to find, difficult to position exactly right, and, unfortunately, they will dry up within a few days—if they even last that long! With these flower hairpins, you will never have to worry about that. You can layer the petals to create a bolder look, or just create a simple everyday pin to wear to school. The flower pins are perfect hair accents for a special event, like a school dance or holiday party. Let's get started!

MATERIALS:

Wide washi tape

Scissors

Small hole punch (optional)

Bobby pin
(or bobby pin base)

Superglue

Gloves

BOBBY PIN BASES

You can find bobby pin bases at most craft stores. These bobby pins have a flat disc attached to them, making it easy to add your designs quickly.

Continued ➡

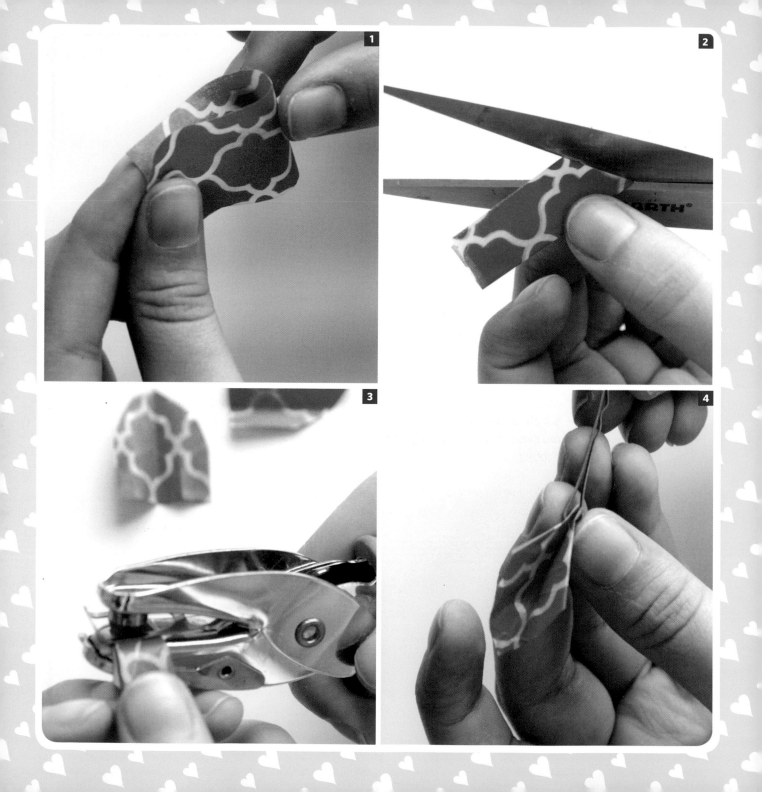

1. Start with a 2"-wide washi tape. Pull out a strip of the washi tape measuring about 2" long, and then fold the tape onto itself so that it measures only 1" and all the adhesive is covered.

2. Fold the strip of tape in half the long way to make it easier to cut, and then cut a half-oval shape for the petals. When you unfold the tape, it should look like a half oval. Repeat steps 1 and 2 about five to seven times, depending on how full you want the flower to look.

3. Make sure the petal is still folded. Using a pair of scissors or a tiny hole punch, cut a tiny circle through the uncut end of the petals. Don't cut it too close to the edge, or the petals may rip when attaching them to the bobby pin.

4. Pull the petals through the bobby pin, one by one.

Continued ➡

5. Use superglue to secure the petals exactly where you want them, if necessary. Superglue can be really messy—and sticky!—so make sure you protect your work area with newspaper, wear gloves, and be careful not to spill any glue. (If your bobby pin has a base for attachments, you can just glue the flower petals on it.)

6. For the center of the petals, just cut out a small strip of washi tape and crumple it up into a little ball.

7. Place the little ball in the middle of all of the flower petals and secure it with superglue.

8. Allow the glue to dry for a few minutes, and your flower is ready to wear!

Bow Ring

Who says bows are just for your hair? These super cute rings make any outfit more fun. Once you've got the hang of making the bows, you can add them to bobby pins or use them to decorate other projects in this book, like the Tin Can Organizers (see Chapter 2: For Your Room).

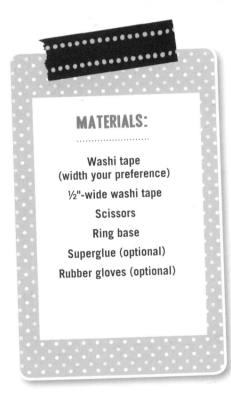

MATERIALS:
....

Washi tape
(width your preference)

½"-wide washi tape

Scissors

Ring base

Superglue (optional)

Rubber gloves (optional)

1. Pull out 8" of washi tape. Once you see how this bow comes out, you can use more or less than 8", depending on what size you want your bow to be.

2. Fold the washi tape onto itself so that you have a 4" strip. Try to get all of the edges to line up, and avoid getting any air bubbles, pockets, or creases.

3. Once you have folded the tape, cut it off the roll with your scissors, and make sure both of the ends are even.

Continued ➡

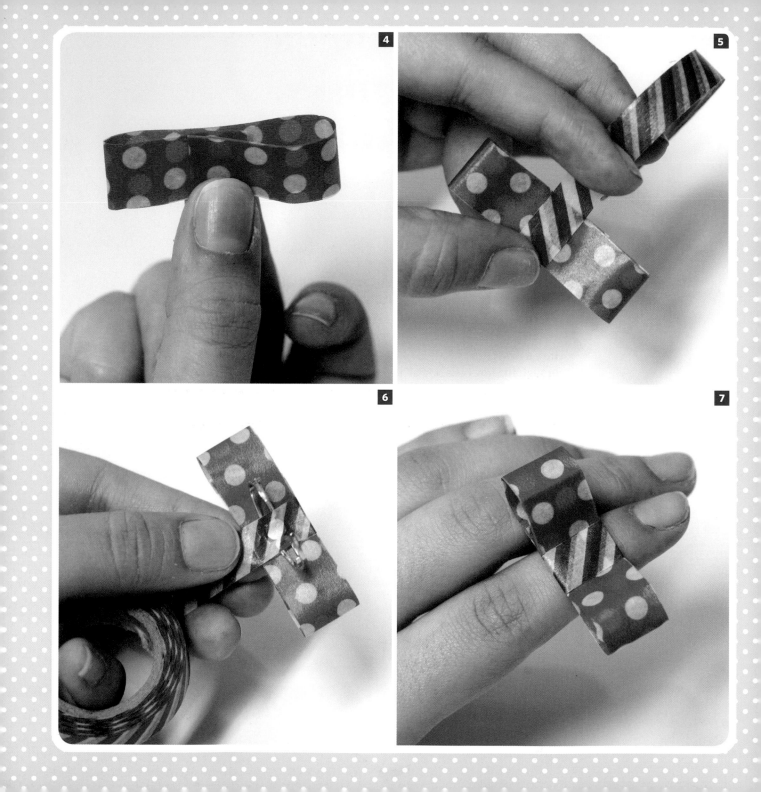

4. Fold the ends of the strip towards the center to make two loops.

5. Use a strip of the ½"-wide washi tape to wrap around the center and secure the loops of the bow in place. This may be tricky at first, but if the loops come undone, just try again.

6. Grab a long strip of your ½"-wide washi tape, and this time wrap it through the ring base and all the way around the front of the bow to attach it to the ring. You can also use some superglue for added security.

7. Once you have wrapped it around a few times, cut the tape and be sure no edges are showing in the front. You are all done!

Barrette

Not a fan of really girly bows? Do you prefer a more simple look for your hair? You can make cute patterned barrettes instead. Like the bows, you can create virtually any color barrette to match your outfit, or give them to friends as gifts. There are tons of ways to spice up the barrettes, too. You can find the white craft foam in bags or sheets at a craft store.

MATERIALS:

White craft foam

Scissors

Washi tape (at least 1" wide)

Mod Podge

Brush

Barrette clip

Superglue

Rubber gloves

1. Cut out a small piece of white craft foam, approximately ½" × 1". You can increase or decrease these measurements depending on the size of barrette you would like.

2. Place your desired washi tape over the strip you just cut out. The foam not only acts as a flexible base, but it also gives the washi tape colors a brighter look.

Continued ➡

TRY THIS!

Want to make your barrette a little more detailed? Use patterned scissors to cut plain tape into interesting layering combinations for a small but super cute variation.

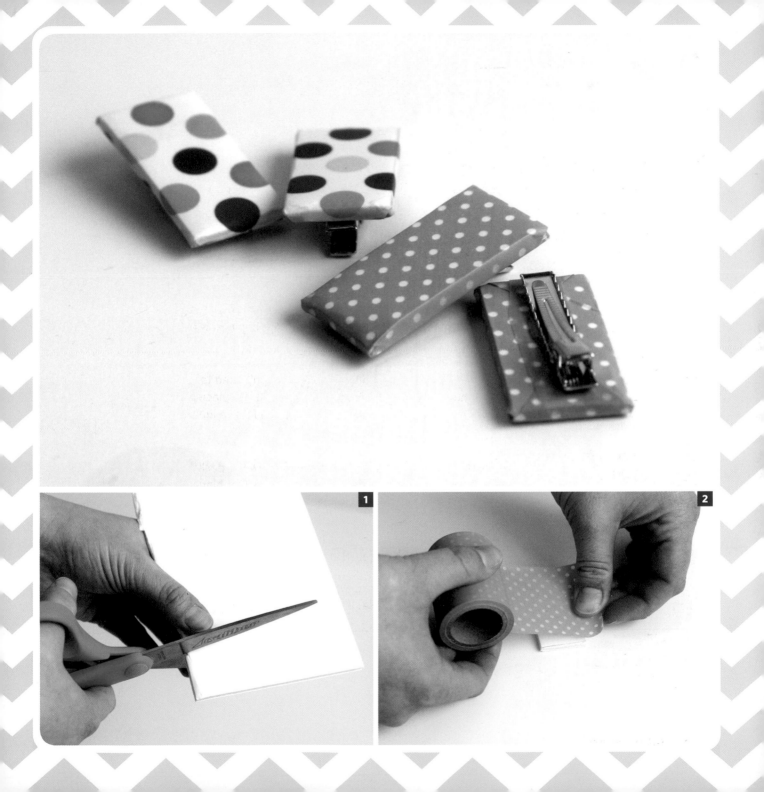

3. Fold any excess washi tape over the edges to completely cover the white foam board. You should only see the washi tape pattern.

4. Since these barrettes might be in your hair daily, it is really important to use a sealer on the design to protect it from wear and tear. Brush on a layer of Mod Podge and let it dry for a few hours.

5. When the Mod Podge is dry, grab some superglue and glue a barrette clip onto the back of the foam board. Superglue can be really messy—and sticky!—so make sure you protect your work area with newspaper, wear gloves, and be careful not to spill any glue.

6. Allow the glue to dry for a few minutes, and your new barrette is ready for use.

CHAPTER 2

For Your Room

TIRED OF THE COLORS IN YOUR ROOM? Are some of your decorations too babyish? Looking for something besides posters to hang on the wall? It's difficult to transform a room without spending money on pricey decorations or messy paint. Believe it or not, there are tons of little ways to change your room into a space that totally reflects your personality and individual style. Changing your light switch plate or adding some frames can totally refresh your room and really make it your own.

In this chapter, you will discover a bunch of cool ideas for redoing all of the spaces in your room. You want your room to be somewhere you can have fun, display your personality, and feel relaxed. Have you picked a color you want to feature yet? Let's get taping . . .

Washi Tape Keyboard

Ever find yourself staring at the keyboard while you're trying to figure out what to type when you're doing some homework for school? Might as well make your keyboard cool to look at! It's time to add some fun to a boring computer area. This will work with practically any computer keyboard. When the tape gets dirty, just replace it! If you want to be able to see through the keys, make sure you use a transparent washi tape.

MATERIALS:

....

Keyboard

Washi tape

Scissors or X-ACTO knife

1. First, disconnect the keyboard from the computer. Prep your keyboard by cleaning out each key, making sure to remove any accumulated dust and grime with a soft cloth.

2. Next, pick the key and type of tape you want to start with, and lay your washi tape over it. (Placing the strip of tape on the keyboard is much easier than measuring out each key with a ruler.)

3. Once you are happy with how it looks, cut the tape along the edge of the key. Try to get the cut as close to the edge of the key as possible.

4. Push down any remaining little corners of the washi tape.

5. Repeat the steps 2 through 4 on accent keys or in any random order you like. You can fill up the entire keyboard, leave half the keys blank, or leave only a few keys blank. Once you have finished decorating, plug the keyboard back in and it's ready to use!

Charger and Cable Markers

Tired of your little sister stealing your charger? Do you live in a family where everyone's got a phone, tablet, eBook reader, and camera, so their cords seem to be all over the place? It can be hard to tell what belongs to whom. Identify your chargers and make them your own with some washi tape. It's something little that can make a huge difference in your daily life, and help you find what you need faster!

MATERIALS:

Cables or phone charger
Various sizes of washi tape
Scissors
X-ACTO knife

1. Start by making sure the charger or cord is completely clean. Use a cloth and a little bit of almost any basic household cleaner to remove dust or grime that may have been left behind by daily use.

2. Pick your washi tape color and design. Start placing your selected colors on your charger or cord. For larger chargers, use wider tapes, leaving the small tapes for smaller chargers and cables.

3. For a more unique look, mix it up with different washi tape selections. You can decorate the chargers with different size tapes and patterns.

4. Have a parent or older sibling use an X-ACTO knife to carefully cut off the excess tape covering the electrical ports. Your charger is all set to use!

TRY THIS!

After you decorate your cords, the rest of your family will probably want to do the same thing! Try assigning a washi tape color to each member of the family to avoid the "hey, that's mine!" arguments.

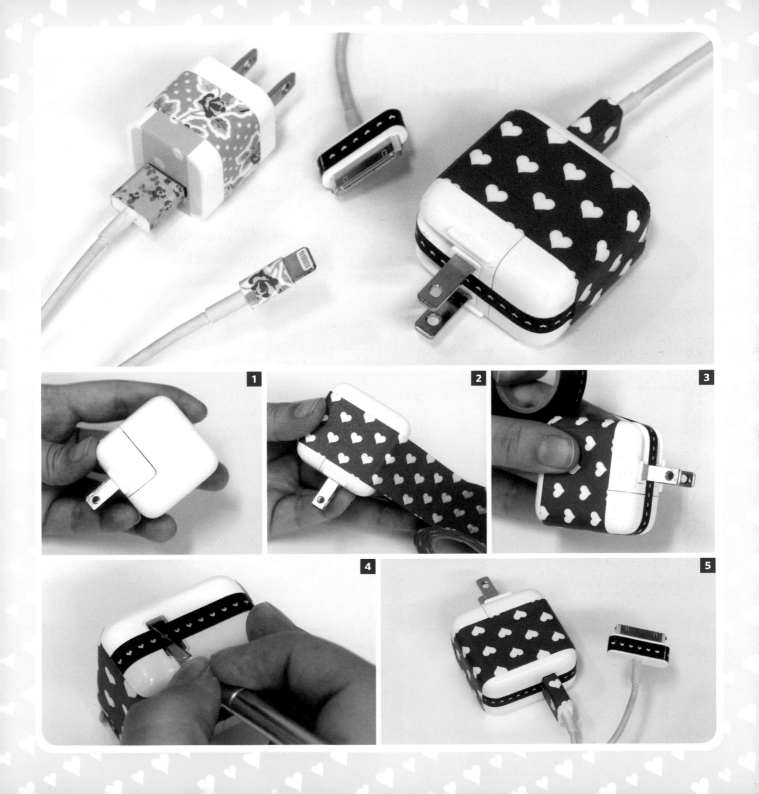

Tin Can Organizer

You don't need to spend tons of money on storage bins when you can make your own cute organizers at home. This tutorial shows you how to make organizers from tin cans, something that you probably have in your kitchen or recycling bin already. Next time you have tomato sauce or soup, keep the cans—you never know when they will come in handy! You can use larger cans for bulkier items and narrower cans for smaller ones.

MATERIALS:

Tin can
Rubbing alcohol
Washi tape
Scissors

1. Start by taking off the lid from your tin can if it's not already all the way off, being careful not to cut yourself with any of the sharp edges. Then make sure your can is completely clean by washing it with soap and water. Have a parent help you take off any remaining adhesives or smells with a cotton ball soaked in the rubbing alcohol.

2. Once the cans are completely clean, allow them to sit for a day to dry completely and get rid of any remaining odor.

3. Now it's time to start wrapping them with washi tape! Start from the top down.

4. Continue to wrap the tin can with different colors and patterns, and cut off any extra washi tape as you go. Repeat this step until you reach the bottom of the can. If you run out of space, just fold over any remaining washi tape toward the bottom of the can.

5. Now that your can is completely wrapped, it's ready to use! Use it to organize your pens and pencils, or any loose accessories in your room.

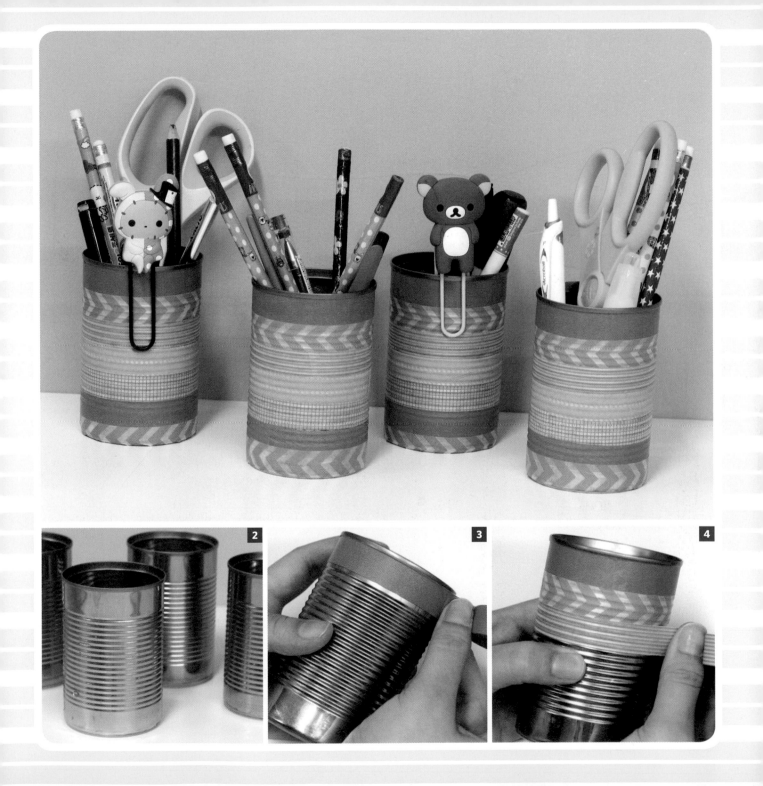

Drawer Organizer

Let's be honest—keeping your room clean is much more fun when you have bright and inviting organizers to keep all your stuff in! It's so much easier to avoid a mess if everything has a place where it belongs. You don't need to spend money on expensive storebought dividers—you can make fabulous drawer organizers yourself! Your parents will be so psyched. Match the drawers with your room décor, or create totally different colored organizers that stand out.

MATERIALS:
....

Ruler

Pencil

Foam board

Scissors or an X-ACTO knife

Superglue

Rubber gloves

Washi tape

Card stock (optional)

1. The first thing to do is measure your drawers, and design what you want your organizer to look like. It helps to divide your supplies and know exactly what you plan to store in each drawer. Take measurements of the length, height, and width for each divider.

2. Grab your ruler and your pencil. Based on your measurements and design, start outlining the pieces you want to cut on a large piece of foam board.

3. Using your scissors or an X-ACTO knife, cut along the lines you drew on the foam board.

4. Once all of your dividers have been cut, make sure that all of your pieces fit in the drawer like you want them to. Once you are happy with how they look, it's time to glue the pieces together.

5. Grab some superglue and glue the pieces together the way you want them to fit in the drawer. Superglue can be really messy—and sticky!—so make sure you protect your work area with newspaper, wear gloves, and be careful not to spill any glue. Allow the glue to dry for a few minutes.

Continued ➡

6. Once all of the glued pieces are dry, wrap them all over with some washi tape to give them a pop of color.

7. This step is optional, but if you'd like to create a bottom for your drawer organizer, it's very simple. Measure your drawer, then cut a piece of card stock the same size as the drawer.

8. Cover this piece of card stock with washi tape, and place it in your drawer.

9. Place the drawer organizers you created over the card stock, and you are ready to go. Happy organizing!

Upcycled Desk

Have an old desk that needs a makeover? Simple. Let's cover it with washi tape! You can customize the desk with prints and colors that match your room. After all, you spend a lot of time at your desk, doing homework and checking Facebook. Why not make it a space that you will love?

MATERIALS:

Old or unfinished desk
Several rolls of washi tape
Scissors

1. Start by making sure your desk surface is completely clean. Ask a parent for help with cleaning the desk—different types of desks will need different kinds of household cleaners.

2. Start layering pieces of washi tape on the table. You don't need to stick to any specific style or pattern if you don't want to. Try placing the pieces diagonally, vertically, or horizontally until you find a look you love.

3. Continue repeating this step until you're happy with how the desk looks. In the design shown, some parts of the desk were kept blank to make a pink and white design. You could cover your entire desk, though.

4. Fold over any extra tape under the desk to avoid the tape peeling off with regular use.

5. Be sure to use coasters for any drinks or liquids on the desk to avoid damaging the tape.

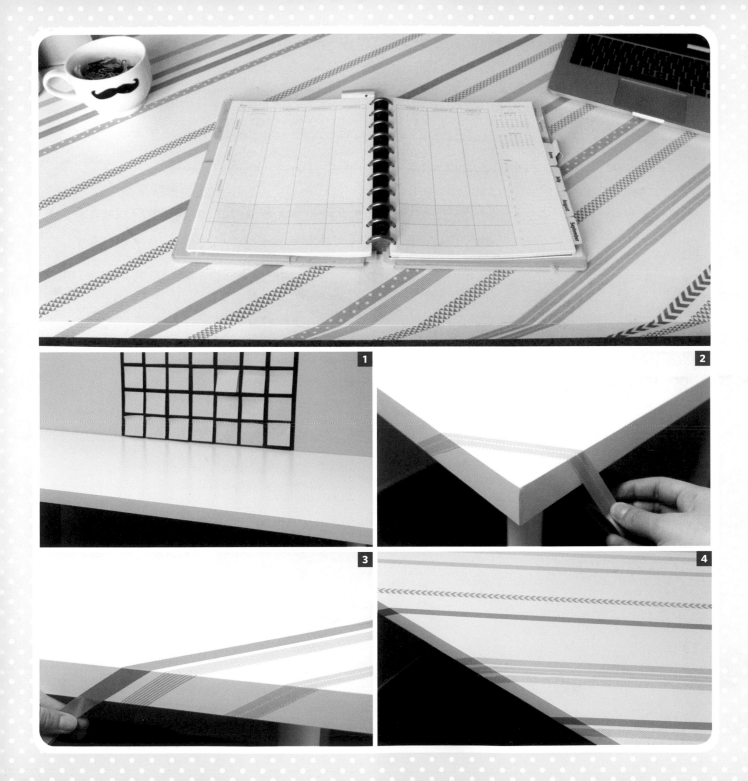

Wall Calendar

Got a lot of tests, sports practices, extracurricular events, or weekend plans? You need a calendar to keep track of everything! The best part of this calendar is that you can grab the Post-it note "day" on your way out the door—you'll be sure to remember everything you need to do that day!

MATERIALS:

Washi tape

Scissors

Post-it notes

1. Place a strip of washi tape horizontally as straight as you can on the wall, leaving space below it for the calendar. This piece of tape is going to be the top border of the calendar.

2. Instead of using a ruler, use the Post-it notes as your measurement guide to create your calendar grid. It will make the process a lot quicker and less confusing. Place seven Post-it notes horizontally under the washi tape to represent the days of the week. Make sure to leave some space between each Post-it note. Place five Post-it notes vertically under the first Post-it note to mark the beginning of each week in the month. Again, leave a bit of space between the Post-it notes.

Continued ➡

3. Place vertical strips of washi tape between the Post-it notes to separate the days of the week. If doesn't matter if it is a little uneven at first. Since washi tape is removable, you can adjust the calendar as you add more Post-it notes.

4. Continue to add rows of Post-it notes under the existing row until you have a total of five rows. Place a horizontal strip of washi tape along the space between each row to finish creating the washi tape calendar grid.

5. On the Post-it notes, write the dates for the month you've created, then add your events or to-do lists. Your calendar is ready to use!

Jewelry Organizer

Mornings are stressful enough. This jewelry organizer will help you save so much time when finding your accessories in the morning! Just grab your necklace and head out. Storing your jewelry in a drawer is just way too messy. It all becomes tangled together and you forget what you even have. This organizer allows you to see your entire collection in one glance.

MATERIALS:
....

Washi tape

Scissors

Pushpins

Necklaces

1. Select a place on your wall where you want to display your jewelry. Start by placing a strip of washi tape horizontally on the wall. Adjust the length of the tape based on how much jewelry you want to display.

2. Place the pushpins on your wall under the washi tape. Don't push the pins flush against the wall if you want to hook multiple necklaces on each pin.

3. Now temporarily hang some of your necklaces on the pushpins.

Continued ➡

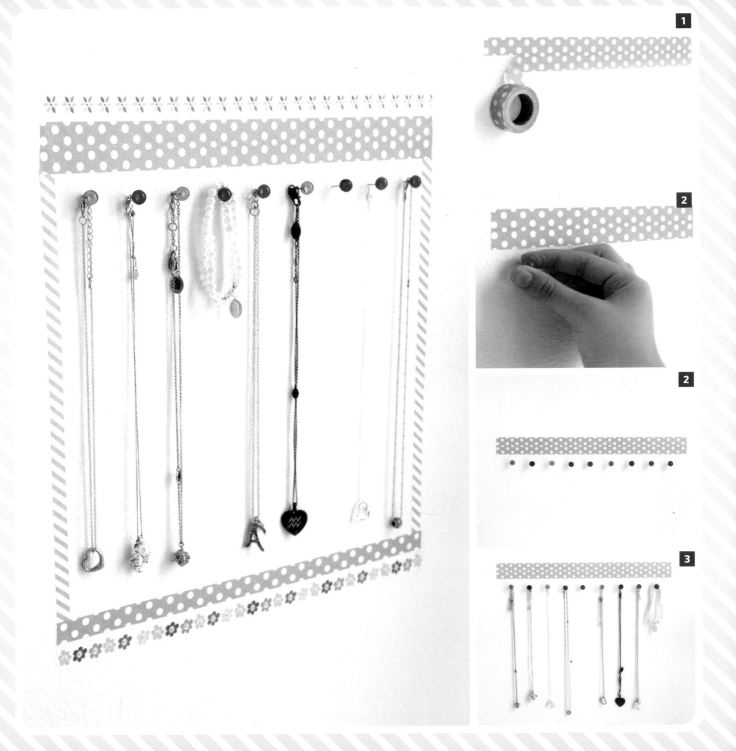

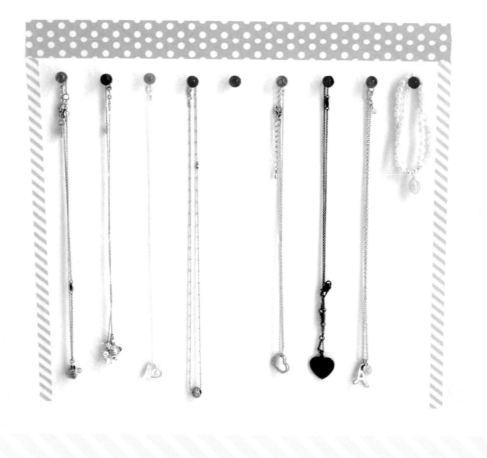

4. Start placing the washi tape on the wall to the right and left sides, based on the length of your necklaces. The washi tape should make a frame around the necklaces.

5. Remove the necklaces while you place the strip of washi tape across the bottom, connecting the two vertical strips. Decorate the frame with more tape. You can create boxes, or simply use another color to outline the frame as a decoration.

6. Once you are satisfied with how the organizer looks, you can hang your necklaces back up, to be used whenever you need them!

Shoebox Upcycle

Have an old shoebox lying around? Why not transform it into an adorable storage bin? If you don't have an old shoebox, you can always buy an unfinished box from any craft store, or ask friends and family to give you any boxes they don't plan to use.

MATERIALS:

Shoebox

White craft paint

Foam paintbrush

Scissors

Several rolls of washi tape

1. First, you want to make sure that the box is as clean as you can get it. Remove any price stickers or adhesives.

2. Start painting the box with white paint. It may take two or three coats for the paint to completely cover the box. Since most washi tapes are translucent, the paint provides a solid background for them; without it, you'd see the logos and designs on the box. Allow the box to dry for a few hours between coats, and after the last coat.

3. Start placing pieces of washi tape over the box diagonally, or in whatever direction you'd like. Tuck the edges of the tape inside the lid and box to hide them. Repeat until the box is completely covered.

Light Switch Plate

Little changes can make a big difference in the overall look of your entire room. This project is a great little accent because you can quickly change it, and if you ever get tired of the color you can remove it easily. You can even add more embellishments, like rhinestones or studs, for a more edgy look.

MATERIALS:

Light switch plate
Screwdriver
Washi tape
Scissors
X-ACTO knife

1. First things first: Grab a screwdriver and remove the switch plate from the wall. You may want a parent to assist or supervise with this process.

2. Once you remove the switch plate, use a household cleaner to remove any dust or dirt from it. Make sure the plate is completely clean and dry before moving to the next step.

3. Start placing your pieces of washi tape over the light plate. Try using colors that match your room, or, for a bolder look, pick a bright accent color that will stand out.

4. Go ahead and cover the hole for the switch; you'll handle that in the next step. Allow the tape to extend past the edges of the plate, and fold them under to help secure it.

5. Working from the front, carefully puncture the tape over the holes for the screws with the tip of your scissors or a pen. Ask a parent to help you cut the hole for the switch with an X-ACTO knife. Fold the tape over the edges of the hole to avoid the tape peeling off later on.

6. Once you have finished folding over the edges, your plate is ready to put back on the wall.

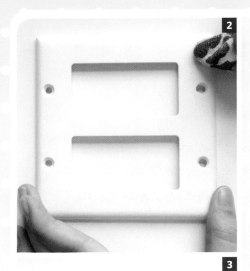

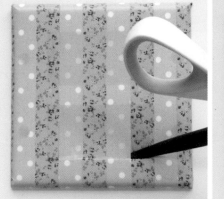

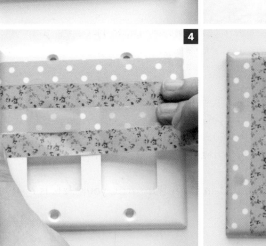

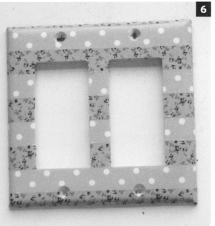

Cutout Art

Sometimes a simple framed print can make a huge difference in how your room looks and feels. This project adds a nice touch to any wall or table. Feel free to make it any size you like; simply adjust the number of "stickers" you make to fill whatever size frame you choose.

MATERIALS:
....

Clear contact paper

Washi tape

Large hole punch in a cool shape, or a stencil

Scissors

Posterboard
(your choice of color)

Frame (your choice of size)

1. Start by cutting out a small piece of contact paper. The contact paper should be big enough to punch your design (or to trace out your stencil) at least three times.

2. Place strips of solid color washi tape over the clear side of the contact paper. Do not place it on the backing.

Continued ➡

3. Cut off any excess washi tape from each edge of the contact paper, otherwise you will not be able to remove the contact paper from the backing.

4. Using your hole punch, punch out your design three times. If you don't have a large enough hole punch, you can always freehand your design or use a stencil.

5. Cut a piece of poster board that will fit into your frame. You can use the inserts from the inside of the frame to give you a guideline as to the size the board needs to be.

6. Before sticking them on, arrange your cutouts on the posterboard until you're happy with their placement.

7. One by one, remove the backing from each cutout, and place the shape on your posterboard. Place the image into your frame, and display it anywhere in your room.

Quote Art

Typography has become an art form in its own right over the last few years. I always keep a few quotes around my room as a source of inspiration. This project is great to keep you motivated or remind you of the important things in life. You can choose the quotes you want, or pick some lyrics from your favorite song!

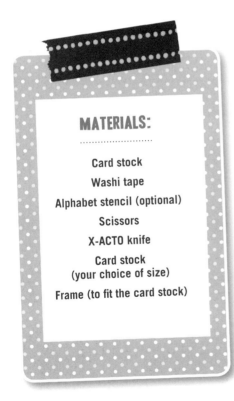

MATERIALS:

Card stock

Washi tape

Alphabet stencil (optional)

Scissors

X-ACTO knife

Card stock
(your choice of size)

Frame (to fit the card stock)

1. Cut out a large piece of card stock. The size you need will vary depending on the length of the quote or saying you want to put on your wall.

2. Place strips of washi tape over the piece of card stock you just cut out. You want the washi tape to completely cover the entire piece.

Continued ➡

TRY THIS!

Use different washi tape designs to make the letters pop.

3. Use a stencil to outline the letters for the quote or saying you want on your wall. You can also freehand the letters if you don't have any stencils available.

4. Ask a parent to help you cut out letters with an X-ACTO knife.

5. Once you have cut the letters, very carefully peel the washi tape letters off of the card stock. Go slowly; you don't want to rip the letters.

6. Place the letters on the cardstock to spell out your favorite quote or saying.

7. Finally, place your picture in a frame and hang it on your wall!

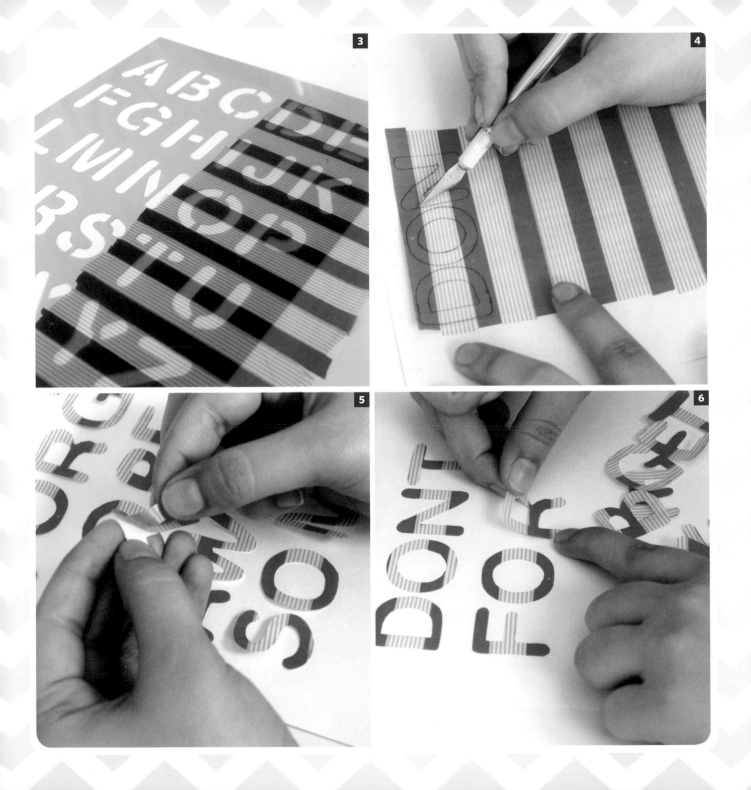

Temporary Wallpaper

Wallpaper is sticky, messy, and hard to remove when you want to change designs. This is a great way to decorate your walls when you want to add a little style, and it won't leave too much of a mess. The best part about it? It's temporary! Remove it when you're ready for something new!

MATERIALS:

Ladder

Washi tape

Scissors

1. Start by making sure the wall is completely clean, smooth and free of any grime or dirt.

2. Ask a parent to help you place the tape on the wall. Have someone stand on a ladder and place the end of the tape flush against the ceiling, while the other person aligns the tape flush against the baseboard or floor.

3. Continue to place pieces of tape on the wall in this way. You can completely cover the wall with tape, or space them apart to create a striped effect.

4. Once you are satisfied with the placement of the tape, run your fingers down each strip of tape to make sure there are no air pockets or bubbles, and that every strip is completely adhered to the wall. Your new wallpaper is done!

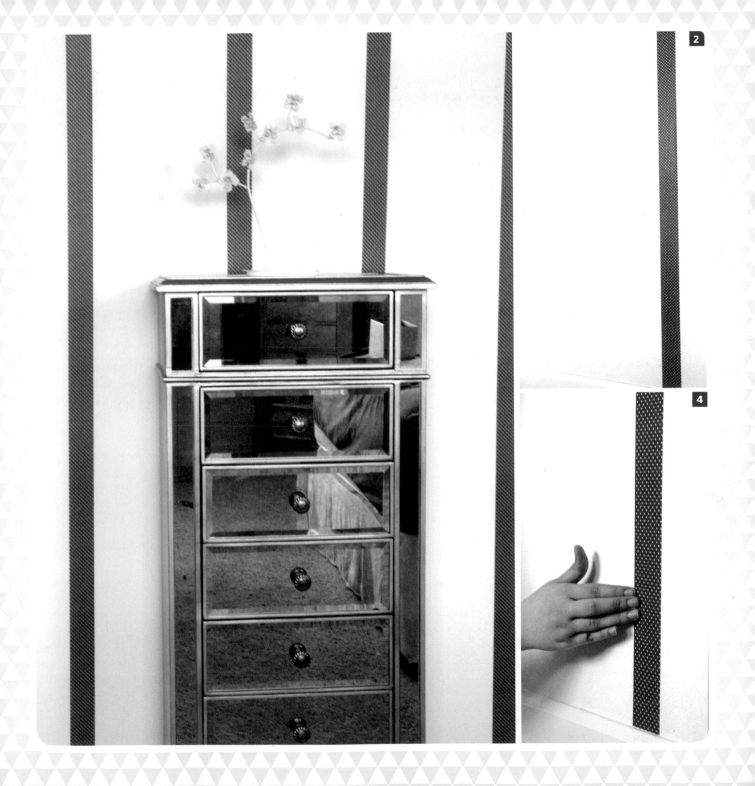

Bed Headboard

Headboards look great, but they can be so expensive. Before you commit to an expensive headboard or furniture set, why not play around with the less expensive washi tape option? You can create lots of different designs that can change whenever you and your room do!

MATERIALS:

Washi tape, thick and thin
Scissors
Ruler or level

1. Make sure the wall is completely clean and free of all dust, lint, and other dirt.

2. Decide how high you want your washi tape headboard to be. Place one strip of tape vertically at each side of the head of the bed, extending from the bed to the height you've chosen. Use a ruler or level to make sure the pieces of tape are placed in a straight line.

3. Once you have placed the tape on both sides, use a horizontal piece of washi tape across the top to connect the two side pieces. Use the ruler or level again to make sure it's straight.

Continued ➡

TRY THIS!

Play with different designs and textures of washi tape. You can create themed landscapes like a park or city, too, instead of a symmetrical design.

4. Using another color of tape, run a piece of tape vertically in the middle of the headboard.

5. Add two more vertical strips of tape on either side of the piece in the middle, breaking the headboard into four even sections.

Continued ➡

6. Begin making a chevron pattern in the two middle sections using thinner washi tape.

7. Continue with the chevron lines until you fill those two sections. Then add two accent pieces of tape to create small triangles in the top corners of the headboard. Or use your imagination and create whatever pattern you like!

CHAPTER 3

For the Holidays

DECORATING YOUR ROOM AND MAKING GIFTS for your friends and family is tons of fun during any holiday throughout the year. These particular projects are also a great opportunity to get the family together for a craft night. Handmade items are always priceless and timeless, and creating them is a great way to spend fun quality time with the people you love. Tell your parents that you are never too old for crafts! They should join in, too.

In this chapter, you will discover cool ideas for a bunch of popular holidays. You can give the finished products to others as gifts, or use them to decorate your own space in a festive way. Try different colors, pattern variations, and embellishments to make each project unique!

Birthday Candle Card

A handmade card is inexpensive and meaningful. This simple design will work for all kinds of people in your life.

MATERIALS:

Blank card (or card stock)

Washi tape
(your choice of
colors and patterns)

Yellow washi tape

Scissors

1. Start with a blank card. You can either buy a pre-cut blank card at a craft store or make one yourself out of some card stock. Buying pre-cut cards is definitely easier (and they come with envelopes!), but if you plan to make a ton of these and you don't mind not having envelopes, it may be cheaper to make your own.

2. Using the colored or patterned washi tape, place vertical strips of different lengths to be the "candles." Line them up with the bases touching the bottom of the card.

3. Cut off a strip of the yellow washi tape. Using your scissors, cut out the flame shape for each candle by hand.

4. Stick the flames on the card above the candles, and your card is ready! Write a thoughtful message inside.

TRY THIS!

Try adding twine, wire, or thread underneath the washi tape candles to give them a more 3D appearance.

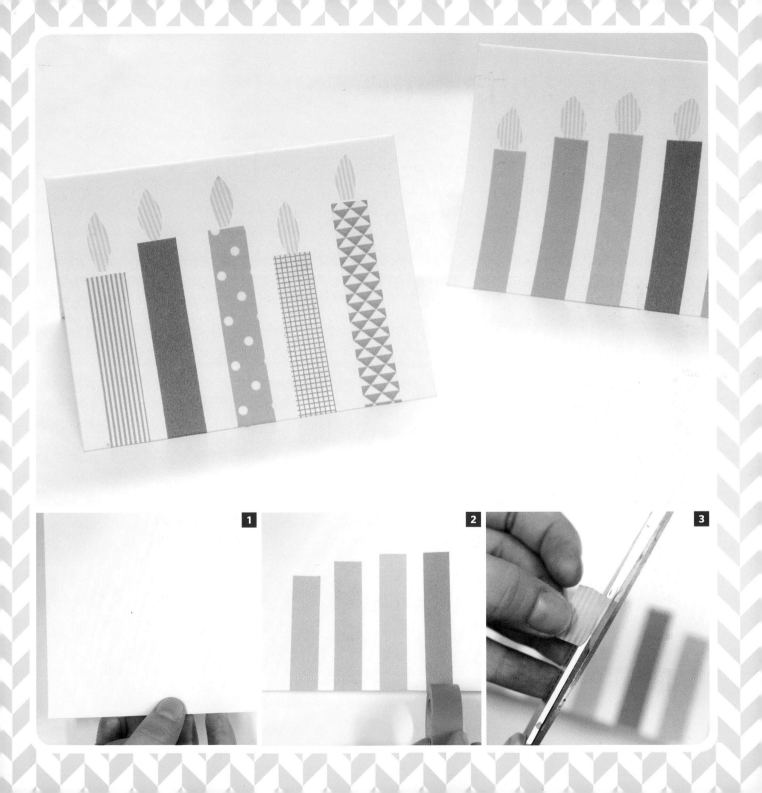

Valentine's Day Card

Valentine's Day is the perfect time to show your loved ones how you feel. Skip the cheesy packaged cards and make your own instead! This modern design is fun and sophisticated at the same time.

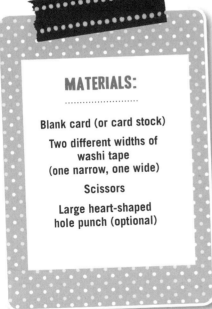

MATERIALS:

Blank card (or card stock)

Two different widths of
washi tape
(one narrow, one wide)

Scissors

Large heart-shaped
hole punch (optional)

1. Start with a blank card. You can either buy a pre-cut blank card at a craft store or make one yourself out of some card stock. Buying pre-cut cards is definitely easier (and they come with envelopes!), but if you plan to make a ton of these and you don't mind not having envelopes, it may be cheaper to make your own.

2. Sketch out an outline lightly with a pencil to mark where you want letters to go.

3. Cut strips of the narrow washi tape to form the letters L, V, and E.

4. Using a heart-shaped hole punch and the wide washi tape, punch a heart to use as the O. If you don't have a heart-shaped hole punch, you can use a pair of scissors to cut out the heart by hand.

5. Place the heart on the card, and adjust the letters if needed.

6. Write a special message inside your card, and it is ready to go!

Valentine's Day Heart Streamers

▲▲▲▲▲▲▲▲▲▲▲▲▲▲▲▲▲▲▲▲▲▲▲▲▲▲▲▲▲▲▲▲▲▲▲

Your school might host a Valentine's Day dance or event that needs decorations. Volunteer this project to decorate any kind of Valentine-themed activity—or your own house! These streamers will set the mood for anything Valentine. They are cheap and easy to make on a tight budget, so make these to your heart's content.

MATERIALS:

Card stock

Washi tape

Scissors

Heart-shaped hole punch or stencil

Small circle hole punch

Twine or craft thread

Tape or pushpins

1. Start with a square piece of card stock. The paper size you need will vary depending on the size of your hole punch or stencil, but you want to be able to cut out as many hearts as possible from it.

2. Start layering pieces of washi tape on the card stock in a random order. In the design shown here, all the hearts are completely unique. You can follow this plan and try to only use each pattern once or alternate between the designs, or come up with your own look.

3. Once you've finished laying down your pieces of washi tape, cut off any extra tape hanging off each side of the card stock.

Continued ➡

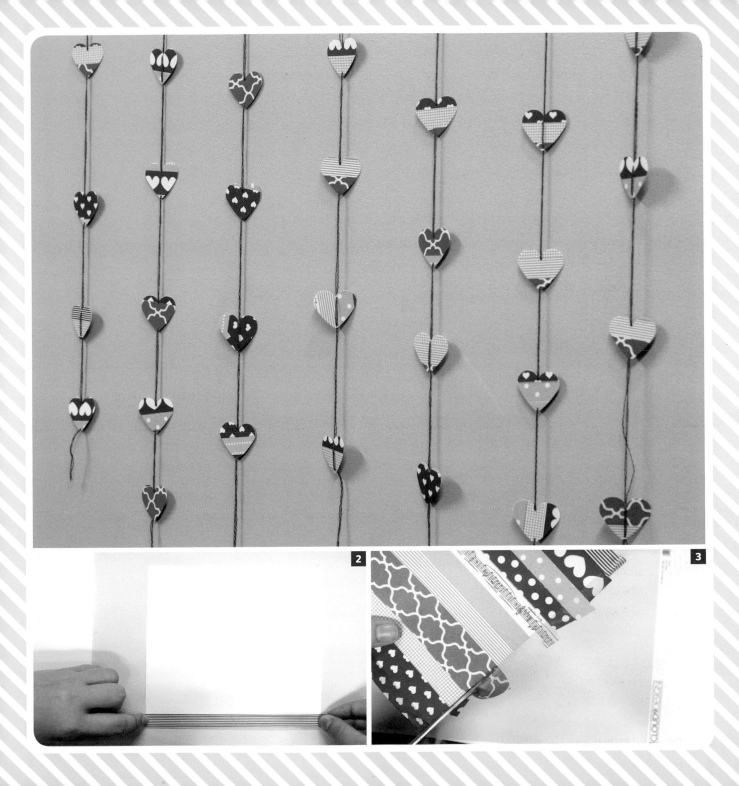

4. Repeat steps 2 and 3 on the reverse side of the card stock, since there should be designs on both sides of the hearts.

5. Next, grab your hole punch or stencil, and cut out as many hearts as you can.

6. Using a small circle hole punch, punch a hole at the bottom and top of each heart. If you don't have a hole punch, try making a hole with a pen or the tip of your scissors.

7. Cut long pieces of twine for each strand of hearts you want to make. (Thread works in a pinch, but the hearts will not hang still like they do with twine.)

8. Loop the twine through the holes in each heart that you punched out.

9. Hang the streamers with tape or pushpins on the wall where you want to display them.

Twist Ties

Making your own gift bags has never been easier. Just grab some wire, washi tape, and some small favor bags. These are perfect for the holidays, birthday party favors, and just for fun! You can customize the colors to match your party or season.

MATERIALS:

Jewelry wire,
any size or weight

Scissors

Washi tape

1. Cut a 1"-long piece of wire.

2. Place the wire on a narrow piece of washi tape. If you don't have a narrow washi tape, you can always cut a wider strip in half length-wise. Leave some extra tape at the ends so the wire can be completely concealed.

3. Place another strip of tape over the wire to cover it completely. Try to get the edges to match up as close as possible. Trim them with the scissors if necessary.

4. Now your tie is ready to be used! Make as many as you need. Twist the ties onto the bags you want to use.

Christmas Matchbox Drawers

Matchbox swaps are very popular these days on websites like Swap-bot. Members of the swaps get assigned a partner and trade supplies, art, or small gifts. It's kind of like being a secret Santa! This matchbox drawer activity really kicks it up a notch. Each drawer can store little knickknacks or even handmade items. You could give a set of drawers to your best friend and fill the drawers with Bow Rings, a Braided Friendship Bracelet, an Initial Necklace, Feather Dangle Earrings, and Bobby Pin Flowers. Or fill the drawers with paper clips, thumbtacks, and magnets and give it to your favorite teacher to say thanks. You can customize the boxes in so many different ways; try adding knobs, bows, or pulls to open the drawers.

MATERIALS:

....

3 matchboxes

Superglue

White acrylic craft paint

Paintbrush

Washi tape

Rubber gloves

Scissors

1. For this project, you will need three matchboxes. Empty out the matches and give them to your parents for safekeeping.

2. Remove the inner slide boxes from the outer sleeves of the matchbox containers and put them to the side for now.

3. Use some superglue to attach the outer sleeves of the matchboxes together. Superglue can be really messy—and sticky!—so make sure you protect your work area with newspaper, wear gloves, and be careful not to spill any glue.

Continued ➡

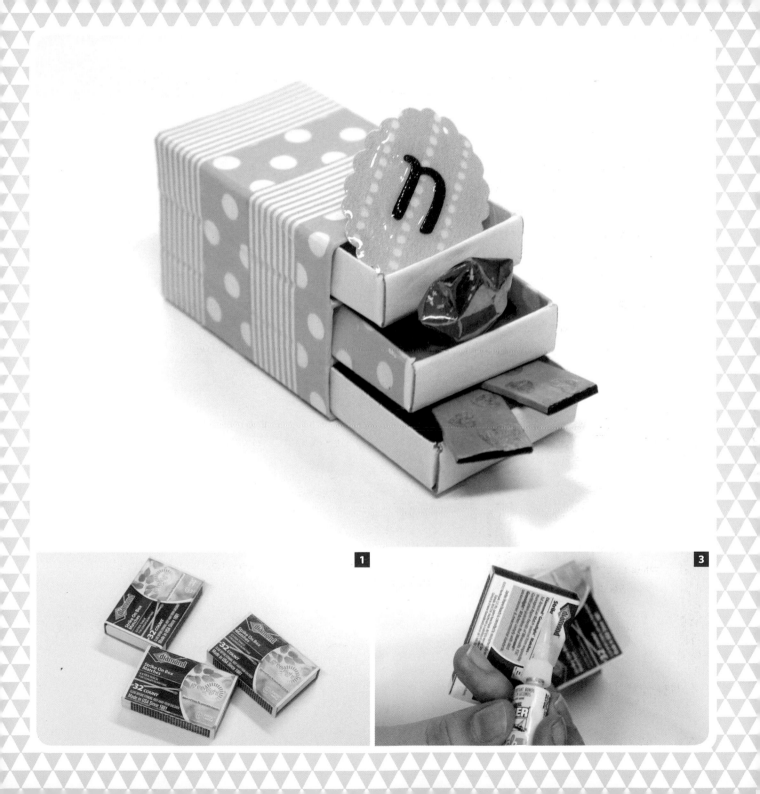

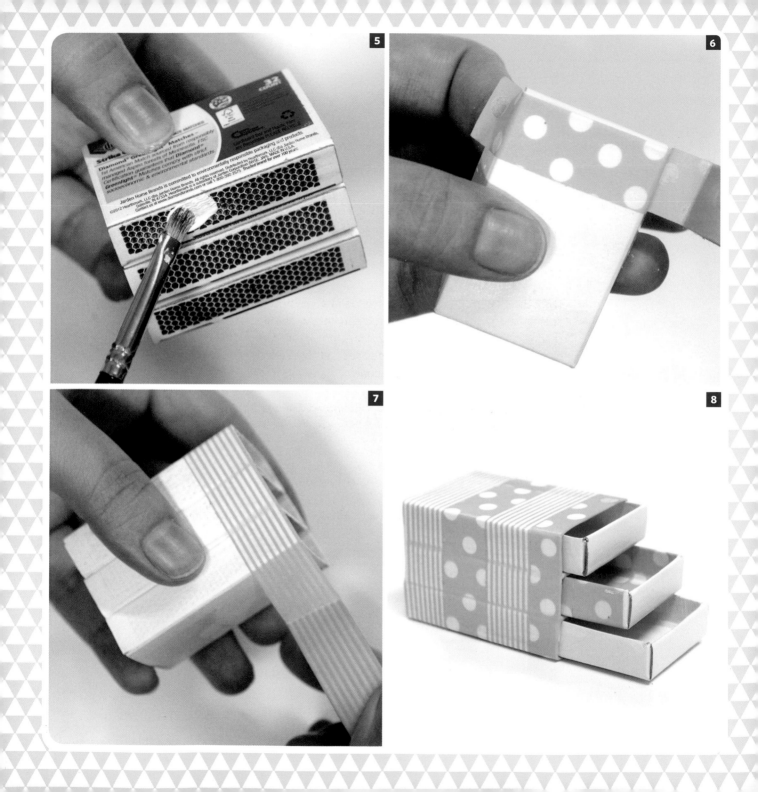

4. Stack the three outer sleeves of the matchboxes on top of one another. Try to make them as straight as possible. To make the drawers, you need to apply superglue to the top of one box sleeve, then stack another sleeve on top. Add superglue to the top of this second sleeve, and place your last box sleeve on top of it.

5. Once the glue is dry, grab your white paint and paintbrush. To avoid seeing the logos and designs from the matchbox through the washi tape, you need to paint the boxes white. It may take two or three coats to completely cover the existing designs. Let the paint dry completely between coats, and after the last coat.

6. Once the boxes are dry, cover the matchboxes with washi tape. The inner "drawers" are usually already white, so all you need to do is cover them with washi tape.

7. Use different patterns to create your own custom design.

8. Your drawers are now ready to use. Fill them with little items as a gift for friends for the holidays!

Candy Cane Christmas Ornament

For many people, the best part of the holidays is decorating and getting the house into the Christmas spirit. Making ornaments is a great family project, as it gets everyone's creative juices flowing and brings the whole family together. These ornaments are so easy to make that everyone in the family can participate. Some other unique ways to customize these ornaments are with glitter, adding some family photos, or using rhinestones to make them sparkle.

MATERIALS:

Foam board

Washi tape

Card stock

Pencil or marker

X-ACTO knife or scissors

Hole punch

Ribbon

1. Start by cutting a square piece of foam board approximately the size you want the ornament to be. This type of board is thick, but still light enough for an ornament.

2. Layer strips of washi tape on top of the foam board.

3. If you plan to make several ornaments, making a template from card stock is the best way to go. Trace a candy cane shape, and cut it out.

4. Trace the candy cane template you just made over the piece of foam board covered with washi tape. Cut the candy cane out with an X-ACTO knife or scissors.

5. Punch a hole at the top of the candy cane with a hole punch. If you don't have a punch, use the tip of your scissors or X-ACTO knife.

6. Loop some ribbon through the hole you just made.

7. Hang the candy cane ornament on the tree. Repeat to make as many ornaments as you would like!

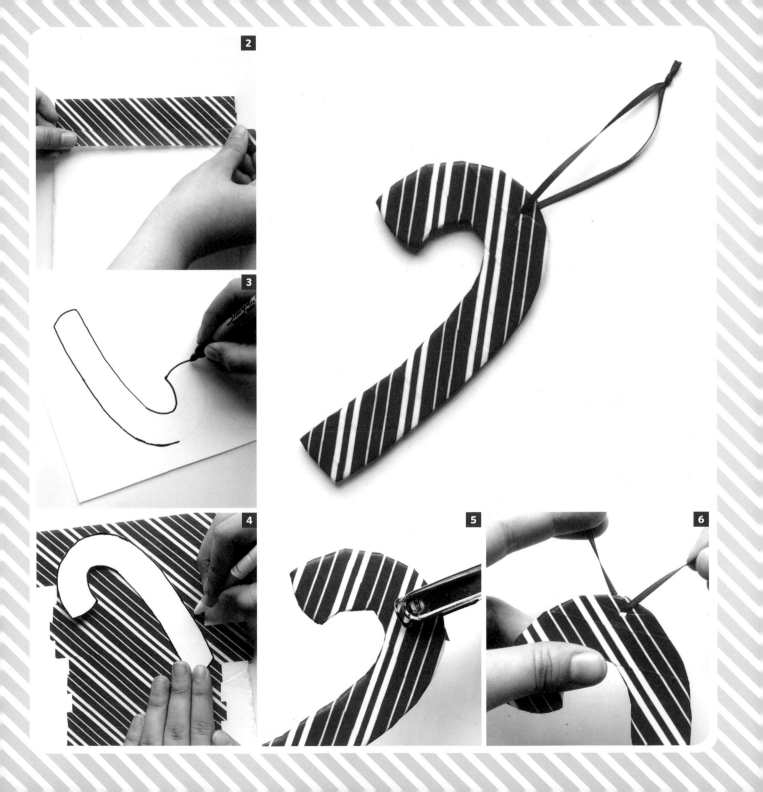

Christmas Tree Card

Many families like to use photos as their Christmas card, but you can branch out on your own if you want—and make a Christmas tree card! There are tons of different card designs you can make with washi tape for Christmas—snowflakes, gift boxes, wreaths, or a sled—but one of my favorites is the washi tape Christmas tree! This design is perfect because it's simple to make, and it's fun to decorate the tree in a variety of ways to make each card special.

MATERIALS:

Blank card (or card stock)

Green washi tape
(in different widths, shades,
and patterns)

Brown washi tape (narrow)

Yellow washi tape (any width)

Scissors

X-ACTO knife

Glue

Buttons

1. Start with a blank card. You can either buy a pre-cut blank card at a craft store or make one yourself out of some card stock. Buying pre-cut cards is definitely easier (and they come with envelopes!), but if you plan to make a ton of these and you don't mind not having envelopes, it may be cheaper to make your own.

2. To create the tree shape, you are going to alternate between different shades of green. Start by placing a strip of tape horizontally one-third of the way up from the bottom of the card. Place the next green strip above it, touching the first strip. Make each strip of tape a bit shorter than the previous one so that your stack of tape strips creates a tree shape.

Continued ➡

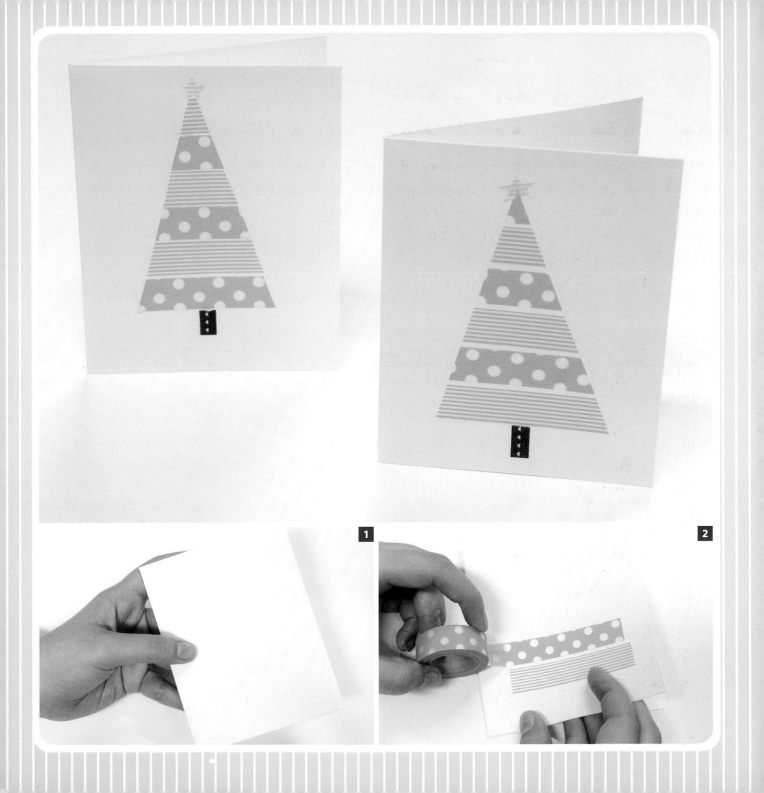

1

2

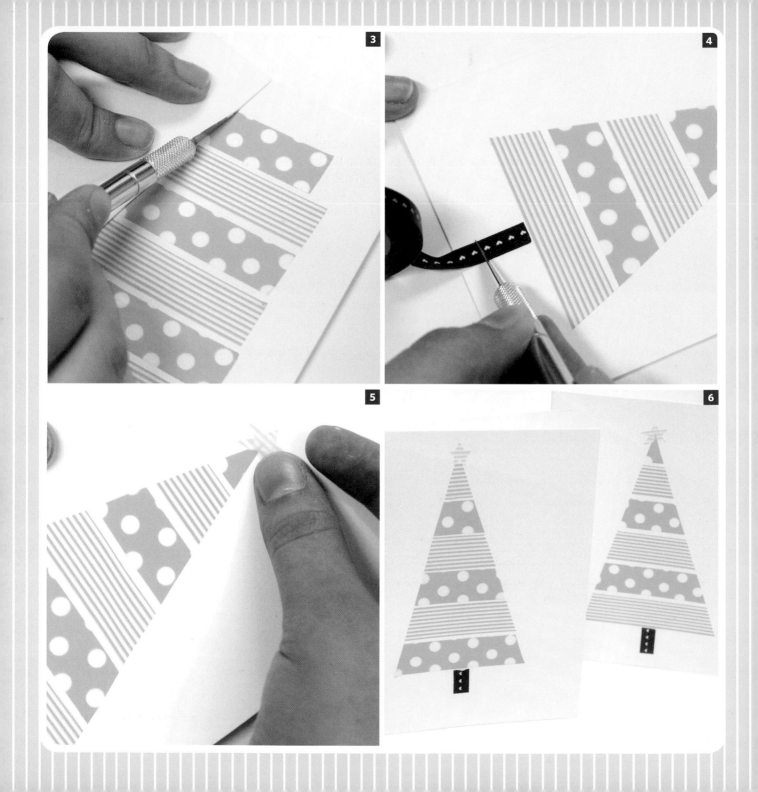

3. Once you have placed all your green strips, grab the X-ACTO knife. Carefully make two small angled cuts in the top green strip, as if you were drawing a triangle shape on the tape. Don't press too hard; you want to cut the tape, but not the card beneath it! Carefully peel away the ends of the tape, leaving the triangle on the top of your tree shape.

4. Cut a small rectangle out of the narrow brown washi tape for the tree trunk.

5. Next, cut a small star out of yellow washi tape. Place it at the top of the tree.

6. You are done! If you'd like to, add ornaments or other details to your tree, or just leave it like this.

TRY THIS!

Making tons of cards for family and friends? Try adding buttons, rhinestones, foam shapes, washi stickers, and other embellishments to make each tree more unique.

CHAPTER 4

For School

SOMETIMES SHOPPING FOR BACK-TO-SCHOOL supplies is more exciting than the actual going back to school part. Checking out aisle after aisle of notebooks, pens, folders . . . so many cool choices! The problem is that some of those fun designs are so expensive. Plus, let's be honest: The more inexpensive options can be super dull and boring. No problem—grab some washi tape and make them better!

In this chapter, you will find plenty of ideas for creating your own personalized school supplies, as well as tons of tips and tricks for getting organized for the new school year. There are plenty of ways to spruce up your supplies, and, of course, you'll use supplies you probably have around your house already. Have a school supply decoration party the week before school starts—invite your friends to come over with their school supplies and some rolls of washi tape. Make some lemonade and get decorating! Time to get started before that morning bell rings . . .

Locker Pen and Pencil Holder

Is it just me, or do your pens always disappear in your bag? You don't want to be that kid who is always asking for a pencil in class. Keeping a fresh stock of pens and pencils in your locker is a great idea. If you are missing a pen, pencil, or highlighter you can just go pick one up from your locker between classes. This locker pen and pencil holder will help keep all of your supplies organized and ready to use.

MATERIALS:

Pencil holder
White paper
Invisible tape
Washi tape
Scissors
Magnetic adhesive sheet

1. Clean off any sticky residue or adhesive left on your pencil holder.

2. A white background means a brighter design. A quick way to get a white background is just to wrap a piece of white paper over the pencil holder. Use invisible tape to secure the white paper.

3. Start adding your washi tape over the pencil holder.

4. Continue wrapping the pencil holder with washi tape until you cover it completely.

5. Measure and cut a piece of magnetic sheeting that covers the back of your pencil holder. Peel off the backing and stick the magnetic sheet to the back of the holder. Now the pencil holder will stick to a metal surface like your locker or refrigerator. Fill it with extra pens and pencils, and you're ready to take notes!

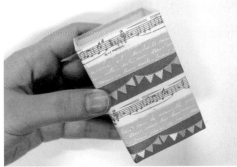

Try This!

Don't have a storebought plastic pencil holder? Make the bottom half of a spaghetti box into a homemade pencil holder instead!

Locker Mirror

You can create a customized mirror for your locker in just a few easy steps. It'll be handy to check how messed up your hair got while you were kicking butt in volleyball in gym class! If you are stuck finding a mirror to decorate, look in a craft store in the glass or candle section, or pop into your local dollar store and check there.

MATERIALS:

Small craft mirror

Magnet adhesive sheet

Washi tape

Scissors

1. Start with a regular craft mirror. You can choose what size or shape you'd like, just make sure it's small enough to fit in your locker.

2. Measure and cut the magnetic adhesive sheet so that it covers the back of the mirror. Remove the adhesive backing and stick it on the mirror.

3. Now it's time to decorate the front. Grab your washi tape and apply strips to the edges of the mirror.

4. Cut off any excess washi tape, and your mirror is ready to use!

Locker Dry-Erase Board

With so many things going on at school, it is easy to forget something. Using a dry-erase board for reminders and to-do lists will definitely help you stay on top of all your assignments and commitments, in and out of school. These boards are really inexpensive to make, which means you can keep one at home and another in your locker at school.

MATERIALS:

Frame with glass

Pencil

Card stock
(your choice of color)

Scissors

Washi tape

Magnetic strips

Glue (optional)

Dry-erase markers

1. Start with a blank frame that will fit in your locker. You can buy unfinished frames at the dollar store, or use an old frame you have lying around.

2. Remove the back of the frame very carefully.

3. Using the back of the frame as a template, trace around it on a piece of card stock.

4. Once you have a clear outline of your frame, cut out the piece of card stock.

Continued ➡

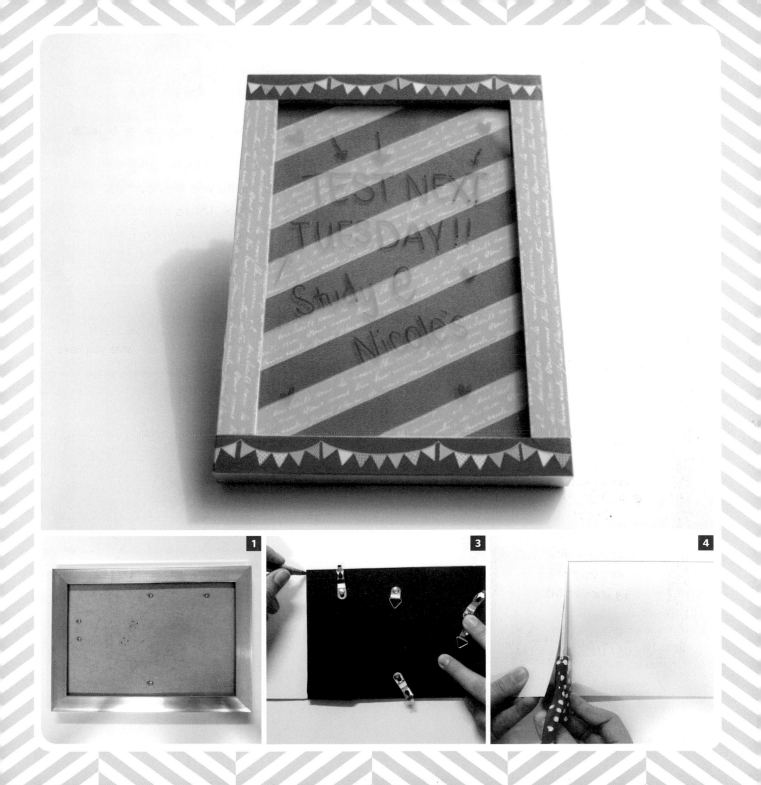

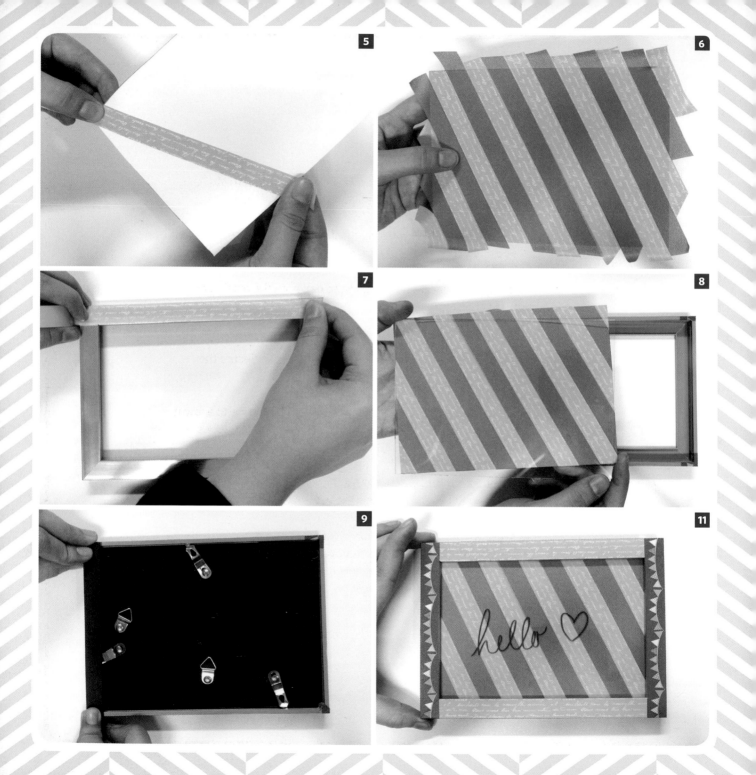

5. Start layering pieces of washi tape over the piece of card stock. Repeat until you have covered the entire surface of the paper.

6. Once you have finished covering the card stock, fold over the extra pieces of tape toward the underside of the card stock.

7. This step is optional, but if you'd like to decorate the outside of your frame, do it now.

8. Put the frame back together, with the piece of card stock you decorated with washi tape serving as the "picture." Secure the frame backing.

9. Add magnetic strips on the top and bottom of the frame to allow it to stick to your locker. If your magnetic strips aren't self-adhesive, glue them on.

10. Turn the frame around so the washi tape "picture" is facing you. You can write anything you'd like on the glass with a dry-erase marker.

11. The board will work pretty similarly to a real dry-erase board—rub the words gently with a cloth to remove the writing.

Magnets

Why spend money on magnets when you can make your own at home? These magnets are really easy to make, and super inexpensive. They make great additions to any locker, but you can use them on any metal surface whenever you need to remember something.

MATERIALS:

Roll of magnetic tape

Washi tape

Scissors

1. To make the magnet strips you will need a roll of magnetic tape. This is a roll of magnetic strip with an adhesive on one side.

2. Cut off a 4" strip of the magnetic tape.

3. Remove the white backing, and place your desired washi tape color over the adhesive of the magnetic strip. Press down to get rid of any air bubbles.

4. Next, grab a pair of scissors and cut the strip into four 1"-sections to create the smaller magnets.

5. Ta-da! You have your own customized washi tape magnets. Use these in your room, locker, fridge, or anywhere else you'd like.

TRY THIS!

Try cutting the strips with textured scissors for a unique look! You can try a jagged cut, waves, or any other decorative edge.

Paper Clip Bookmark

It is so hard to stay organized when you have tons of things going on at school. These are perfect for keeping track of important pages in a textbook or notebook. You can easily flip to where you left off, or to key points you need to study. Create a color scheme that goes with all your school supplies, or designate a color scheme for each class!

MATERIALS:
....

Paper clips

Scissors

Narrow washi tape

1. Take a look at your paper clip and decide how long you want the flag to be. Cut a piece of washi tape twice that length. Loop your washi tape through the paper clip until the paper clip is about halfway between the ends of the piece of tape. (If you don't have narrow washi tape, cut a wider piece of tape lengthwise for two narrower pieces.)

2. Carefully stick the two ends of the tape together, sandwiching the paper clip in the fold of the tape. Try to line up the edges and avoid bubbles.

3. To add a quick little design to the bookmark, cut a diagonal line through the tape.

4. Now your new bookmark is ready to use!

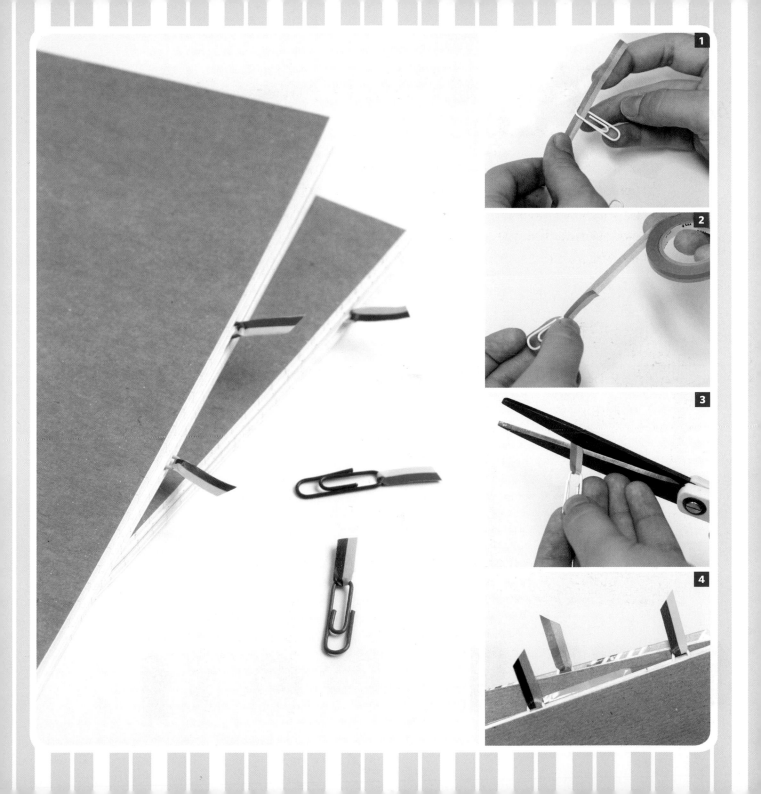

Cloud and Raindrop Bookmark

If you want a more creative alternative to the standard rectangular bookmarks, these are a perfect idea. This bookmark will help you remember where you left off and will make you smile whenever you see it—rain or shine!

MATERIALS:
....

Card stock

Washi tape

Small hole punch

Scissors

Narrow ribbon

1. Start by cutting out a square piece of card stock. It doesn't need to be a super precise size—just big enough to create your cloud shape later.

2. Place strips of washi tape over the card stock. You can use a patterned tape or a solid color tape.

3. Cut off any excess tape from the sides, and cover the back of the card stock with strips of washi tape.

Continued ➡

TRY THIS!

There are many other combinations and variations to this design. See what kind of designs you can think up! Here are a few to get you started:

❋ Soccer ball and net

❋ Bacon and eggs

❋ Bunny and carrot

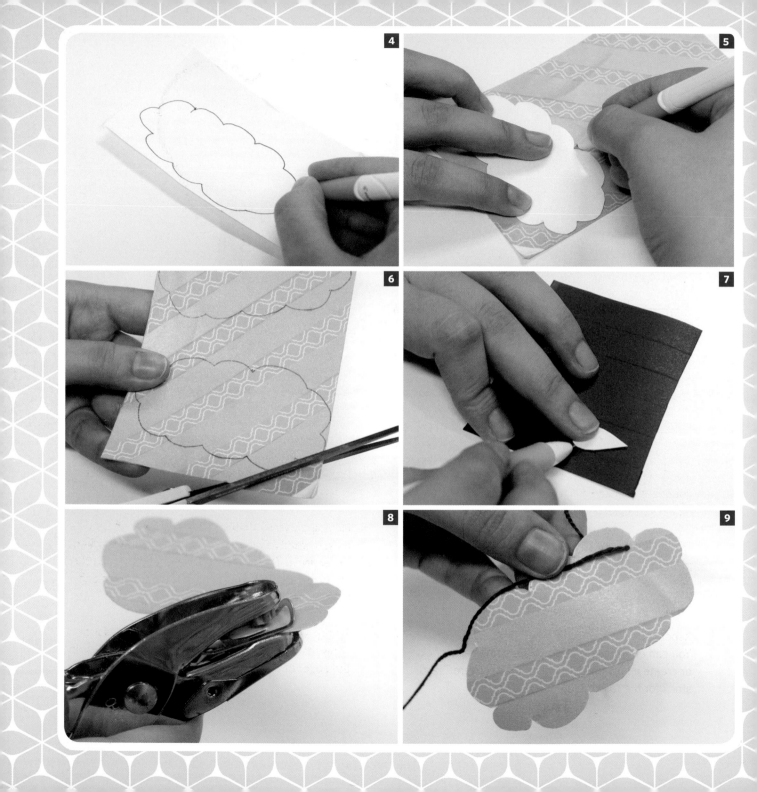

4. If you plan to make several cloud bookmarks, it's a good idea to make a cloud template. Draw a cloud on a regular piece of paper and cut it out.

5. Trace the template over the washi tape–covered piece of card stock you created earlier.

6. Cut out the cloud(s) from your card stock.

7. Repeat steps 4 through 6 with a raindrop shape. You can either use a scrap of the same card stock, or create a new piece of washi tape–covered card stock for the raindrop.

8. Once both designs are cut out, punch small holes in both the cloud and raindrop.

9. Next, grab your narrow ribbon and cut it about 6" long. Thread it through the cloud and tie a tiny knot to secure it. Then thread the other end through the raindrop and tie another tiny knot there, to attach both pieces together.

10. Finally, your bookmark is ready to use. The cloud stays inside the pages, and the raindrop dangles on the cover of the book.

Pencil Case Roll

Are your pens and pencils hiding at the bottom of your backpack? This pencil case is perfect for storing all of your supplies while you're on the go. No more digging through your backpack or asking your friends to borrow a pencil again! You can make this pencil case with just a few simple materials.

MATERIALS:

Paper towel roll

White paint

Paintbrush

Scissors

Foam board

Pencil

Superglue

Rubber gloves

Card stock

Washi tape

1. Start with a clean paper towel roll. Make sure you remove any traces of paper or glue as best you can before you begin.

2. To make the colors of tape show up a bit brighter, paint the entire roll with white paint. Allow the paint to dry for a few hours before proceeding to the next step.

3. Cut the roll in two, about a little bit more than halfway. You want to make sure your supplies will fit in one side of the roll, while the other side will be the "cap."

4. Take your piece of foam board. Using a pencil and the bottom of your paper towel roll as a template, draw two circles to cover the open holes in the bottom and top ends of your pencil roll. Cut out the two circles.

Continued ➡

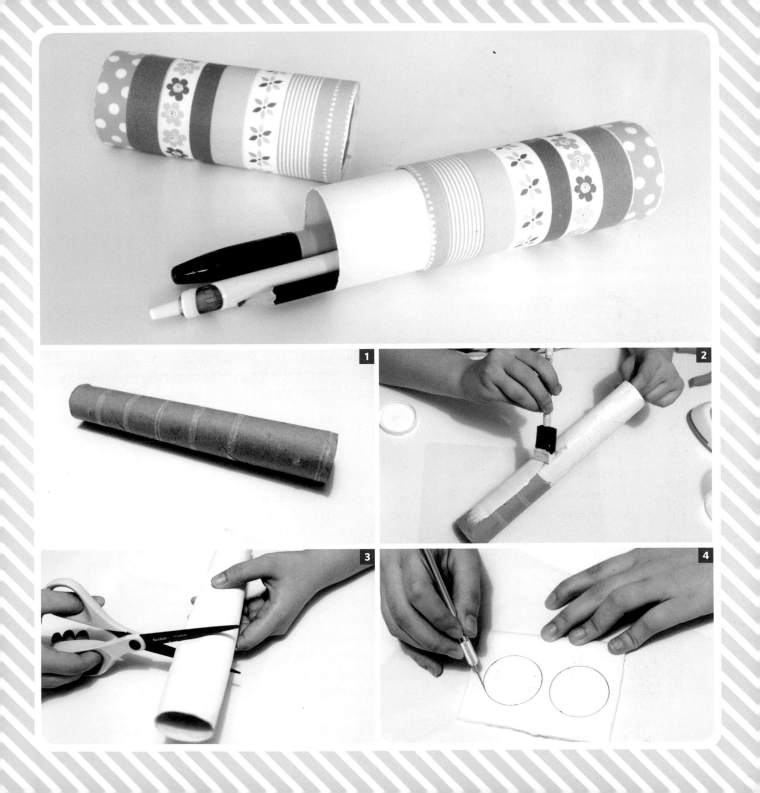

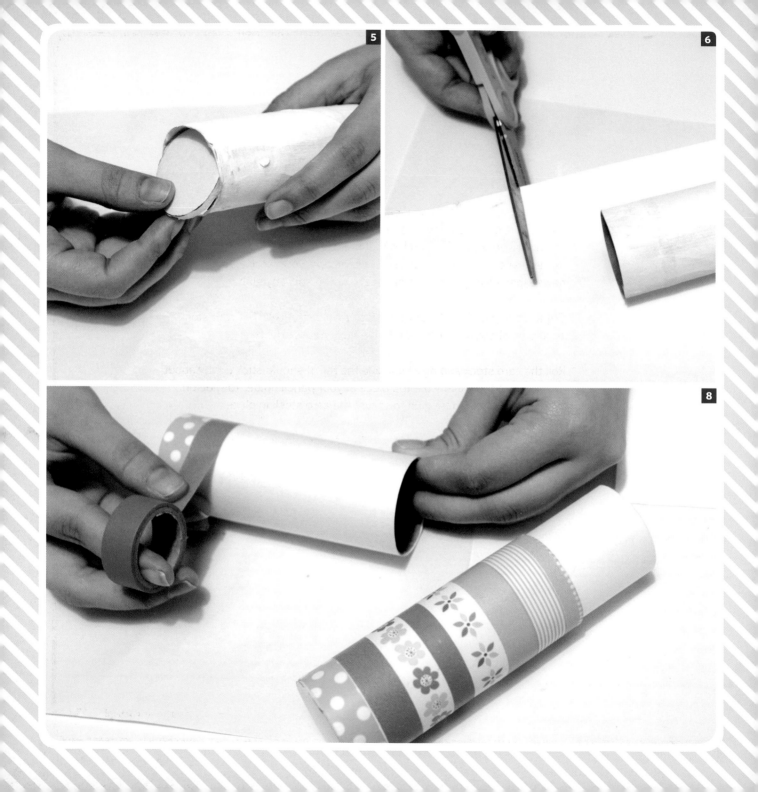

5. Glue one piece of foam board on the top of one piece of the roll, and at the bottom of the other with some superglue. This step is necessary to make sure your pens don't fall out of the roll. Superglue can be really messy—and sticky!—so make sure you protect your work area with newspaper, wear gloves, and be careful not to spill any glue.

6. Cut a rectangle of card stock to fit inside the larger roll. The card stock should be about one inch longer than the length of the roll.

7. Roll the card stock and place it inside the roll. It should stick out by about one inch. This will allow the top piece of your pencil holder to slide on and close perfectly. Use glue to secure the card stock in place.

8. Cover the roll with the washi tape colors of your choice.

9. Once you are finished decorating, it's time to put your supplies in your new pencil roll!

Washi Tape Pens

Pens are one of the most basic school supply items. They come in a million different varieties, from basic and boring to chic and expensive! You can actually create your own bright and colorful pens from those boring, basic ones in just a few minutes. For the price of one fancy pen, you can buy a whole pack of blank pens and decorate them yourself. This idea can be modified for any kind of pen; just use your imagination.

MATERIALS:

Pens with clear casings

Washi tape

Scissors

1. Start by very carefully removing the ink cartridge from the casing of the pen. Pull the writing tip carefully; the ink cartridge should come out easily with a little pulling.

2. Make sure you do not remove the tip from the cartridge itself. This will cause the ink to spill out and create a mess. Set the casing aside.

3. Pull out a piece of washi tape about the length of the ink cartridge, and place the tube on top of the strip. Don't place the writing tip on the tape. Cut off any excess tape.

4. Wrap the strip of washi tape around the cartridge of ink. For lighter tapes, you may want to wrap the tape around twice.

5. Carefully replace the ink cartridge back in the clear casing and close it up again. Enjoy your newly customized pen!

TRY THIS!

Placing the tape at different angles totally changes the look of the pen. Experiment with other options! Also, you could cover the outside of the pen itself.

1

2

3

4

5

Washi Tape Pencils

There is nothing more boring than a yellow number-two pencil. You can create a cool color scheme for your pencils to match your backpack or other school supplies. This project is pretty simple, but, as always, you can spice it up by mixing up the colors and adding other embellishments to the pencils. They might even bring you extra luck on your tests!

MATERIALS:

Pencils

Washi tape

Scissors or X-ACTO knife

1. Start with your regular number-two pencils. Any type of pencil will work for this project.

2. Starting from the eraser tip, begin wrapping the washi tape around the pencil in a spiral.

3. Wrap it around the pencil completely. Remove any excess tape at the eraser or tip with an X-ACTO knife or scissors.

4. Repeat steps 2 and 3 with as many pencils as you want. Try creating color schemes that will match your other school supplies!

5. When you are sharpening your pencils, make sure that you sharpen in the opposite direction that your tape is wrapped, so the tape doesn't come off. As long as you do this, the tape should stay in place!

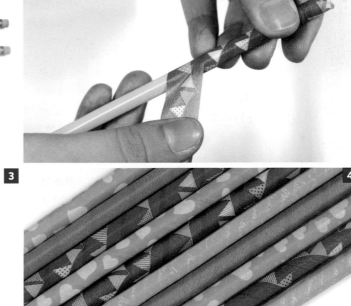

Supply Labels

You don't need an electronic label maker; you can make your own labels with your name on them at home. This is such a fun project, because you can create tons of different colored labels to match your school supplies. Washi tape is generally translucent, but for this tutorial I really suggest you use a lighter color. Tapes with bold patterns or darker colors tend to not show up as well.

MATERIALS:

Printer
Paper
Washi tape
Scissors
Waxed paper

1. The first thing you want to do is print a sheet of paper with the names or words you want to make labels with. Just type the words into a word processing document in the size and font you want, and print them out.

2. Lay a piece of washi tape over the words.

Continued ➡

Ashley Ashley Ashley Ashley Ashley
Ashley Ashley Ashley Ashley Ashley
Ashley Ashley Ashley Ashley Ashley
Ashley Ashley Ashley Ashley Ashley
Ashley Ashley Ashley Ashley Ashley
Ashley Ashley Ashley Ashley Ashley
Ashley Ashley Ashley Ashley Ashley
Ashley Ashley Ashley Ashley Ashley
Ashley Ashley Ashley Ashley Ashley
Ashley Ashley Ashley Ashley Ashley
Ashley Ashley Ashley Ashley Ashley
Ashley Ashley Ashley Ashley Ashley

1

2

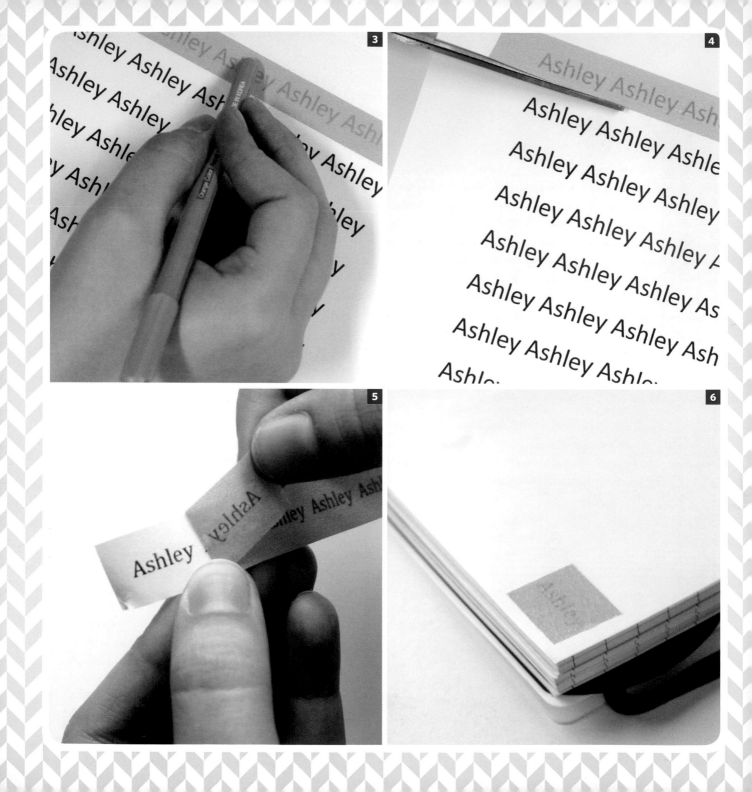

3. With your finger or the rounded end of a marker, rub the tape over the words to allow the ink to transfer onto the tape.

4. Cut out the strip you just made, making sure to trim any excess tape you don't want on the labels.

5. Peel the tape off the paper very carefully, so that the paper doesn't stick to the tape.

6. Cut out the individual labels and place them on your supplies. Keep any remaining labels on a sheet of waxed paper for future use.

Organization Labels

Getting organized for school is one of the keys for success. With these labels you can keep track of all your binders, folders, and projects. This will help keep all of your assignments organized so you don't have to rummage through your bookbag any more.

MATERIALS:

Contact paper

Washi tape

Scissors

Waxed paper

Large hole punch (optional)

1. Start by cutting out a square piece of contact paper big enough to punch out a few labels. This may vary depending on what you are organizing; for smaller folders and notebooks you only need a small piece.

2. Place strips of washi tape over the contact paper. Use a lighter color tape; it will allow you to see the words you'll write on it more easily.

3. Punch out some labels from the washi tape–covered contact paper with your hole punch (if desired). If you don't have a large one, just cut out any shape you want with your scissors.

4. Place the labels on any surface you want to organize. Write on your labels just like regular paper. However, keep in mind that these labels won't unstick, since you're using contact paper.

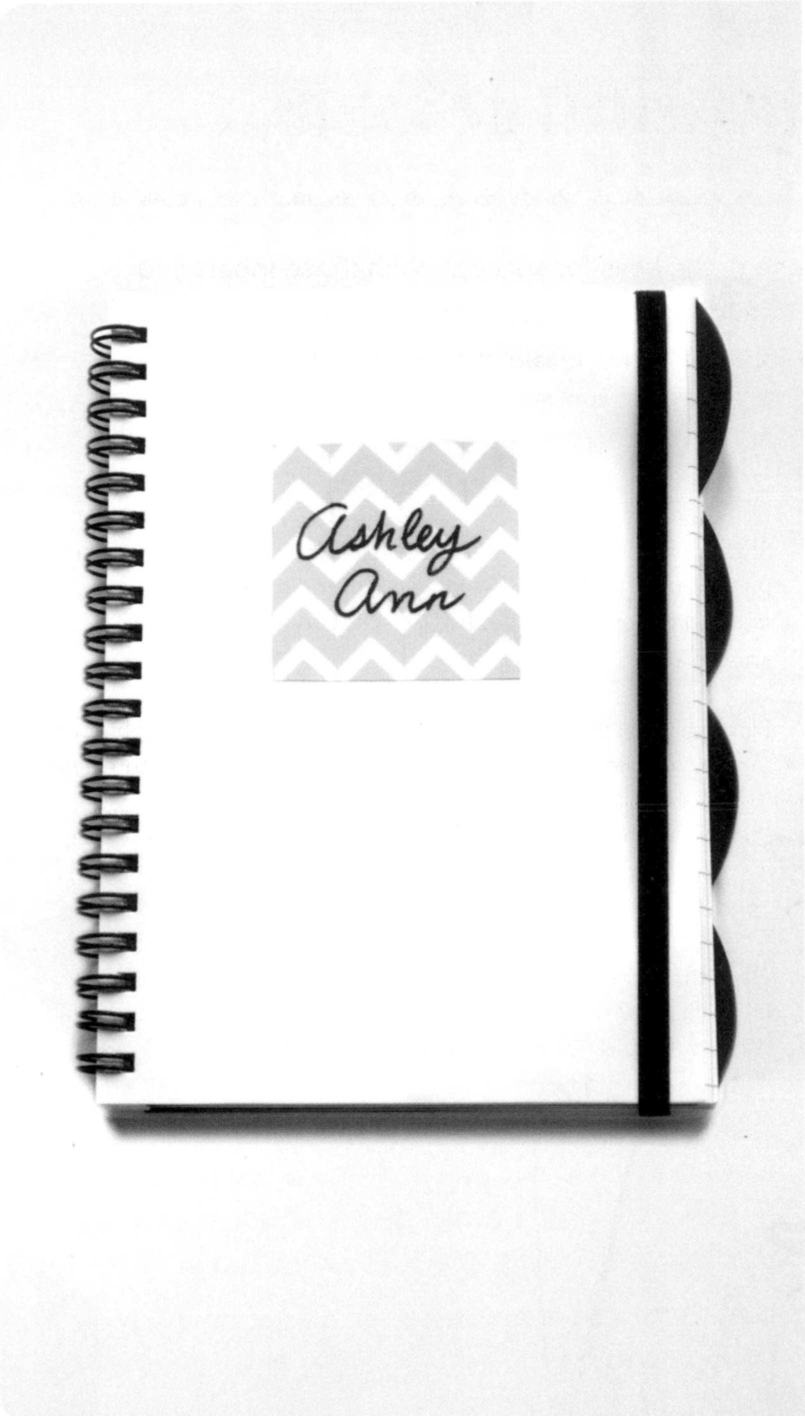
Ashley
Ann

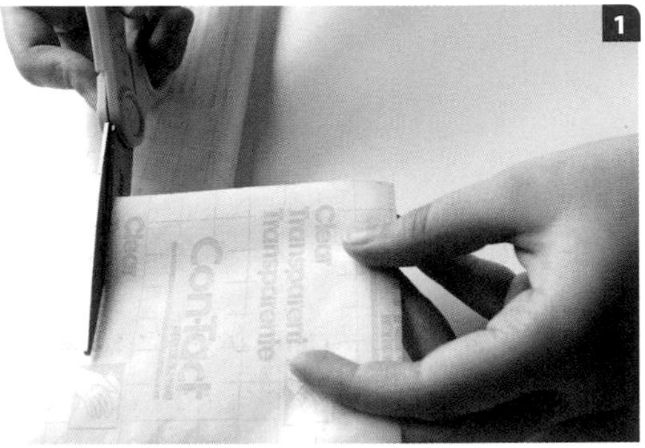
1
Clear
transparent
transparente
Con-Tact

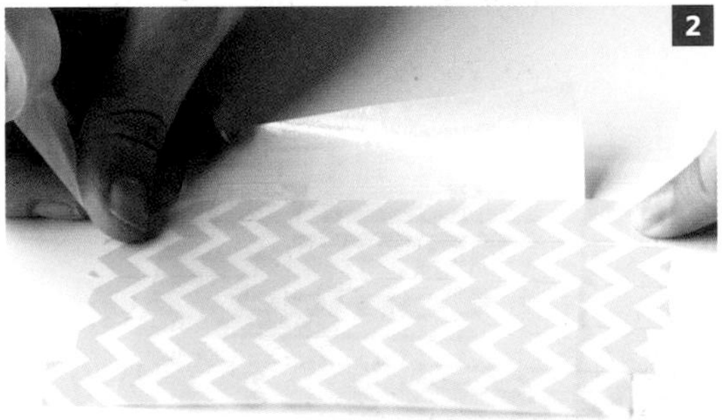
2

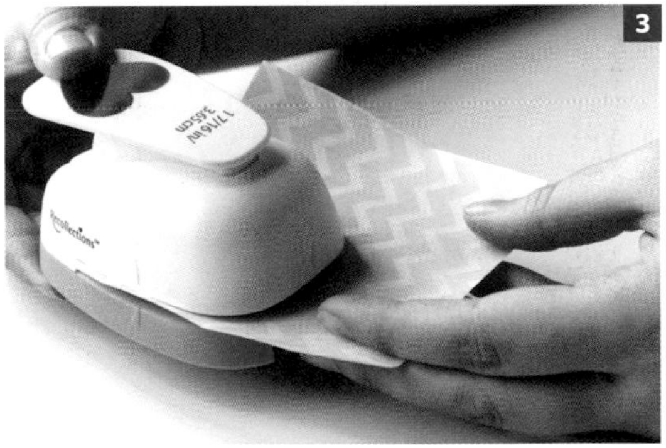
3
1 7/16 in
3.65cm
Recollections

4
Ashley
Ann

Textbook Cover

Most schools these days require that students use book covers to protect their textbooks, since another student will probably use it next year. But that doesn't mean it has to be one of those solid-color boring covers like everyone else has! Creating a washi tape book cover is really easy, and just takes a few steps. Covering the book first with brown paper is the cheapest method (you can usually find a roll of the brown paper in most dollar stores), but if you can't find it, a brown paper bag from the grocery store works just as well.

MATERIALS:

Brown paper (or paper bag)

Ruler

Pencil

Scissors

Sheet of paper

X-ACTO knife

Card stock

Washi tape

Invisible tape

1. Wrap the brown paper around your book to get an idea of how big a piece you'll need for the cover. Using a ruler and a pencil, outline the areas where you want to make cuts. You want to make sure you leave at least 1" extra on every side of the book so you are able to fold it inside the covers later. Once you have created your lines, cut out your cover.

2. Put the paper cover to the side for a moment while you design the silhouette image you want on the front cover of your book. You can either create your own shape on a sheet of paper, or download and print a design from the Internet. Cut out your design to use as a template.

3. Place your template on the brown paper cover, where you want the design to be. Trace the design onto the brown paper.

Continued ➡

4. Cut your silhouette out of the brown paper very carefully. If you want, have a parent help you cut the design out with an X-ACTO knife.

5. Grab a sheet of card stock, and cut out a square slightly larger than the hole where you cut out your silhouette.

6. Cover the piece of card stock with washi tape, using the colors and patterns you want to show up in the hole you cut out.

7. Fold the excess washi tape over the sides of the card stock, or cut it off.

8. Tape the card stock square under the design you created on your cover.

9. Finally, wrap your book with the brown paper, fastening it inside the front and back covers with tape.

TRY THIS!

Stuck on what design to make? Search online for images using the keyword "silhouette," and you will find tons of options. Some of my favorite designs to make are bunnies, flowers, stars, cats, and elephants.

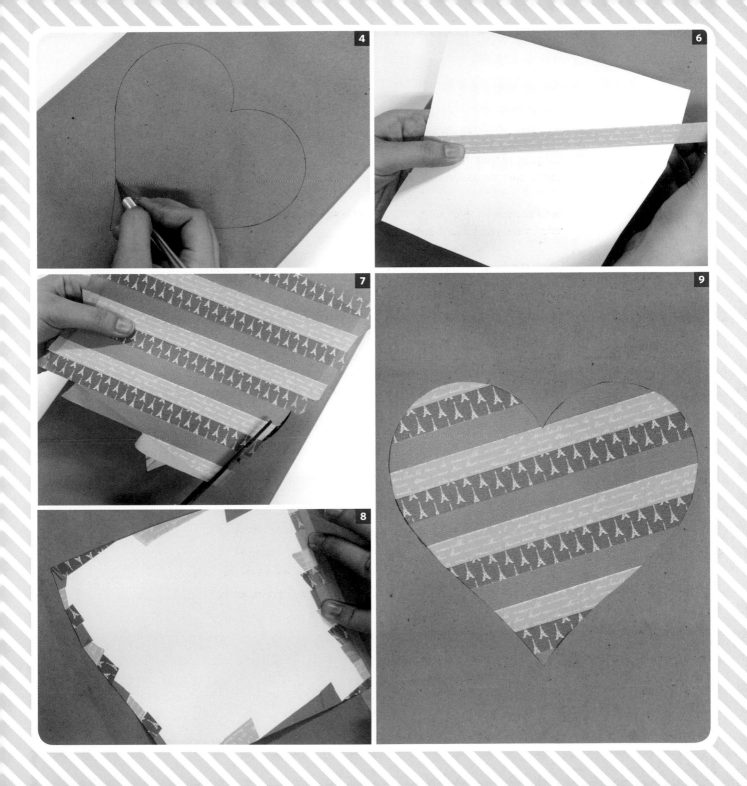

Composition Book

Most composition books come in the standard black color. How boring is that? By decorating yours with washi tape, you will be sure to stand out in a sea of boring notebooks. Who says you can't be smart *and* stylish? You can mix it up with different prints and patterns to show off your unique style in the classroom.

MATERIALS:

Composition book
White paper
Scissors
Invisible tape
Washi tape

1. Since you can see through washi tape, you will first need to cover the composition book with white paper. Grab some basic white copy or printer paper and wrap it around your composition book to help cover the black.

2. Tuck any extra paper inside the notebook covers, and secure it with invisible tape.

3. Now, grab your washi tape and start applying strips to the notebook, alternating patterns.

4. Keep applying strips of washi tape until the entire notebook is covered. Fold any extra pieces of tape under the cover of the composition book.

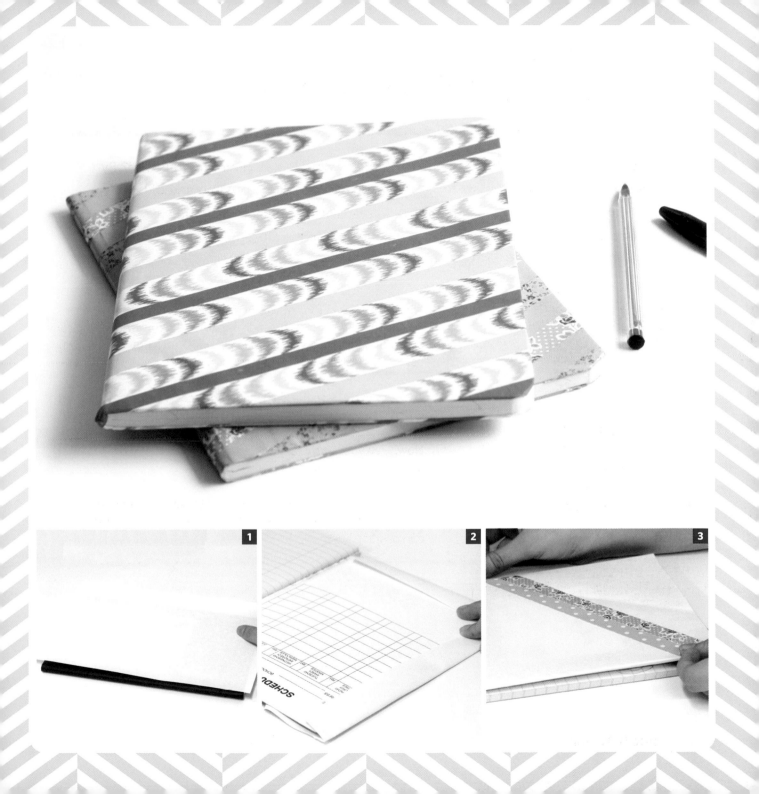

Washi Tape Stickers

Yes, you can make your own stickers! It's simple to do, and you can store them on some waxed paper for later. This is a great project for washi tape that has little standalone pictures on it (rather than a pattern or plain color)—but you can make shapes out of any tape you want! Use them on a homemade card, journal, planner, or anywhere you'd like to add a touch of fun.

MATERIALS:

Scissors

Washi tape with little pictures on it

Waxed paper

1. Pull out a strip of your washi tape with the images you would like to use as stickers.

2. Use your scissors to cut out your stickers very carefully.

3. Store your unused stickers on a square of waxed paper.

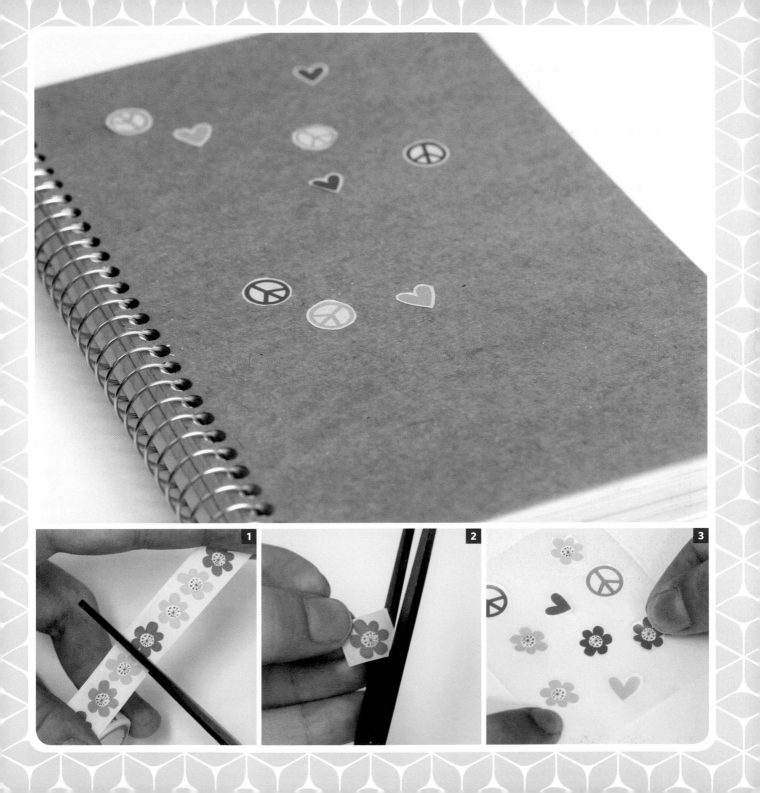

Index

About the Author

Ashley Ann Laz is the creator of the popular YouTube craft channels PaperPastels (*www.youtube.com/user/ PaperPastels*) and Sweetorials (*www.youtube.com/user/ Sweetorials*). Ashley has been crafting her entire life, and has worked on everything from ceramics to scrapbooking. She specializes in cute projects you can make quickly.